The *Promise*
of
Kierkegaard

Other Works by Kenneth Hamilton

What's New in Religion?
John Updike: A Critical Essay
J. D. Salinger: A Critical Essay
In Search of Contemporary Man
God Is Dead: The Anatomy of a Slogan
Revolt Against Heaven: An Enquiry into Anti-supernaturalism
The System and the Gospel: A Critique of Paul Tillich
The Protestant Way
Life in One's Stride: A Short Study in Dietrich Bonhoeffer

The Promise of Theology
Martin E. Marty, General Editor

The Promise
of
Kierkegaard

by

KENNETH HAMILTON

J. B. LIPPINCOTT COMPANY
Philadelphia and New York

Foreword

Modern Christian thought is too diverse to be able to claim a single father. But Søren Kierkegaard was the inspiring genius behind the largest number of contemporary Christian approaches and themes. It is proper to begin a series of books on modern theology with him.

After a century of relative obscurity, Kierkegaard was rediscovered by existentialists and crisis theologians; by the end of World War II, devotion to his thought had reached faddish proportions. An inevitable but minor reaction set in.

Today we are free to see Kierkegaard in perspective, compelled neither to belong to his cult nor to cover up our ties to his influence.

As Professor Kenneth Hamilton demonstrates, Kierkegaard's vision of his own time can serve to guide men in our similarly unsettling age. His ideas have by no means been exhausted, his challenge to complacency has rarely been faced—in short, as the title implies, he is still ahead of us, still full of promise.

Those who have read much recent philosophy or theology should welcome the opening brief review of the Danish author's life as a preparation for the fresh presentation of his ideas and their consequences which follows. Relative newcomers to his thought may wish to begin with the Epilogue and, after Chapter I, interrupt with Chapter IV. In this sequence, they can begin to see how directly Kierkegaard speaks to a later day; this should prepare them to move on to the second and third chapters, which are necessarily somewhat more demanding. Beyond this, as editor, I shall stay out of the way of the author's own argument. It makes sense. Kierkegaard would have liked that. It does not make "system." He would have liked that, too.

MARTIN E. MARTY
The University of Chicago

Contents

[7]

What may betide me in the immediate future I know not; how it will be in the following age when I have passed into history, that I know.

— *The Point of View for My Work as an Author*

Introduction:
He Will Not Stay Put
in Copenhagen

SØREN AABYE KIERKEGAARD was born on May 5, 1813, and died on November 11, 1855. Both events—and nearly everything in between—took place in Copenhagen, Denmark. He became engaged, but never married. Instead he wrote. He wrote as if possessed by a demented demon with a sense of humor. His sole subject as an author, he said, was Christianity. Also he admitted he had taken some pains to make the reader work this out for himself.

He made a few brief visits to Berlin and a journey of filial piety to West Jutland, where his father, Michael Pedersen Kierkegaard, had been reared in poverty before he became a prosperous wool merchant owning a big house in the capital. Otherwise he hardly strayed outside Copenhagen and its environs, although he complained loudly about the frustrations he suffered by being "a genius in a provincial town." It was a love-hate relationship on both sides. Copenhagen smiled on her gifted son by recognizing, almost from the time he started writing, the genius he claimed for himself so confidently and so rightly; then she showed another side of her nature and went out of her way to make his life miserable. After his death the rest of Scandinavia began to hear about this unusual Dane, and already in the 1860s Henrik Ibsen in Norway was drawing on his work for his own purposes. Kierkegaard's preoccupations are evident in Ibsen's *Brand* and, less directly, in *Peer Gynt.*

His impact on the wider world was rather like that of a series of time bombs. In the 1890s some philosophic circles in Germany "discovered" him, thus bringing to pass the event he had foreseen with distaste, namely, that he would eventually fall into the hands of "the Professors." But the full force of his original mind was not felt in German-speaking Europe until after World War I, when the impression it made was largely responsible for triggering two separate intellectual movements of the first importance: crisis theology and existentialism. In Switzerland and in Germany, theologians Karl Barth and Emil Brunner and philosophers Karl Jaspers and Martin Heidegger, between them, claimed Kierkegaard as one of the giants of nineteenth-century creative thought, the equal (if not the superior) of a Marx or a Nietzsche or a Dostoevski.

As usual, the Anglo-Saxon public caught the Continental fever after a time lag. It was not until the mid-1930s that the first book in English about Kierkegaard came on the market. By the early 1940s his works began to arrive in English translation with a rush. Kierkegaard was "in." And, if intellectually pretentious persons did not know exactly why any more than their neighbors, the mere mention of the name—especially if pronounced "Kër-kë-gaw" in would-be Danish fashion—was impressive. After World War II and the publicity given Jean Paul Sartre and his café philosophy, things became a little easier. It was always safe to refer to Kierkegaard as the "father of existentialism."

Today the long list of Kierkegaard's writings is almost completely available in English, while critical studies abound. Thanks to the work of Kierkegaard scholars of many nations, his thought stands out much more clearly than it did even a short while back. For example, any paternity suit brought against him now for fathering existentialism would be likely to be promptly dismissed.

Kierkegaard gives delight, but he also irritates. Once in his childhood, rebuked at table for overloading his fork, he replied saucily, "I *am* a fork, and I will stick you." "Fork" became his name in the family after that. A fork he still remains, prodding his reader in defiance of all the rules in the etiquette book for authors; and, when we are stuck by him, we know it. We then wish he had remained in decent obscurity in Copenhagen, his authorship buried beside him. Unfortunately for our complacency, he will not stay put there. The eddying, unpredictable waters of his sentences, with their deadly undertow of logic, sweep away the fashionable clichés we use to hide the poverty of our ideas, leaving us feeling rather ridiculous. Yet, somehow, we keep on reading.

I

The Crucible
of the Authorship

ONE OF THE MANY EPIGRAMS in Benjamin Disraeli's novels runs this way, "Read no history; nothing but biography, for that is life without theory." Although Disraeli and Kierkegaard were contemporaries (Disraeli being born nine years earlier and outliving the other by more than a quarter of a century) and although both were authors, wits, and men of imagination possessing a strong belief in their own capacities, their outlook on life was as unlike as it is possible to imagine. Yet the shrewd, successful man of the world and the semirecluse who said of himself, "I live in the isolated cabin of melancholy," had this in common: *a strong sense of the claims of the actual over against the ideational and the ideological.* This made Disraeli a formidable figure in politics. And it put iron into Kierkegaard's presentation of Christianity.

All the same, biography would not have appeared to Kierkegaard as theory-free, since he knew only too intimately from his own experience the distance between the outward event and its inward significance. Life without theory he found rather in Shakespeare, whom he praised for his "objectivity" (C.I., 336).* Nevertheless, biographical data remain the best pointers we have to the truth about another human being, even though the "life" we reconstruct with their aid is necessarily a theoretical affair, and quite possibly remote from reality. In connection with Kierkegaard, we may hope, the attempt to tie significance to event may not be a wasted effort. He himself has

*See page 111 for the key to abbreviations referring to Kierkegaard's writings.

left us so many autobiographical comments he must have wanted us to make something of them.

His "crazy" upbringing—that is the subject to which he continually returns. Theodor Haecker's book *Kierkegaard, the Cripple*[1] draws attention to the way in which a deformity of the spine (thought to be the result of a fall) warped Kierkegaard's life. But even when in 1846 the satiric paper *The Corsair* published a series of caricatures making fun of his unequally matched legs, and so exposing him to public ridicule, Kierkegaard's anger was over the psychological rather than over the physical aspects of this exposure. His small, ungainly frame, together with his perpetual ill health, he accepted forthrightly enough as a discipline of suffering to be endured. His memories of his home life were not so easily or so stoically accepted. There was an ambiguity here that, probe as he would, he could not resolve.

No one can doubt that in these memories is the key to Kierkegaard's career. Not only was the child the father of the man, as always happens more or less; but the child lived on in the man, even consciously so. Kierkegaard tells us that he had never really known childhood, that he had been all his life an old man. It was little wonder, then, that to the last he was still trying to deal with the problems he had agonized over as a small boy, seeking and never finding an easement for his early puzzlements and terrors. His whole authorship, indeed, was forged in the crucible of those experiences, just as the whole course of his life was directed by them.

Everything went back to his father, who ruled him in life and from the grave. Søren was the youngest of seven children, his father being fifty-seven when he was born, his mother forty-five. The age of his parents might have meant much or little and would in any case have been expected to make a bright boy overly precocious. But Søren discovered that he had come into a home given over to death; and he never believed otherwise than that the destiny of the home (his father's house), once he had been born into it, was his destiny for ever. An entry in his *Journals* reads:

[13]

It seems as though I were a galley-slave, chained to death; every time life moves the chains rattle and death withers everything—*and that happens every minute* (Dru, 136).

His discovery of the shape of the dark and terrible cloud of death emanating from his father and overshadowing the household came only in his early manhood, and then not all at once. The *fact* of the cloud he knew long before, as we learn from the reminiscence he set down in his *Journals* (Dru, 483). His father once, watching his small son sit mute and unhappy, remarked: "Poor child, you are living in a silent despair." The boy, we are told, felt that the father spoke chiefly to himself; and so father and son remained united in a common misery requiring no words of explanation between them.

The actual course of Søren's progressive uncovering of the cause of his father's "silent despair" is difficult to trace. The evidence is scattered through the *Journals,* which he began to write casually when he was twenty, took up seriously a year later, and from then on continued through his career. But the *Journals* were never diaries, and their writer's firm intention to cover his tracks—so far as the intimate details of his family life were concerned—resulted in cryptic references to events that touched him deeply being made, often years later, without any hint of their historical context. Such journal entries, indeed, were likely to turn up again, rewritten and further disguised, in his books.

The first revelation seems to have occured in 1835 when Søren had been five years at the university (where he went at seventeen). It is recorded in the *Journals* in 1844:

A relationship between father and son, where the son secretly discovers everything after, yet dares not acknowledge it. The father is a respectable man, severe and God-fearing, only once in a state of intoxication he lets drop a few words which hint at the worst. Otherwise the son does not discover what it is and never dares ask his father or others (Dru, 503).

Apparently his father had married his mother, a relative, who at the time of the first wife's death was acting as a servant in

[14]

the house and was five months pregnant. That Søren knew enough about his father's guilty remorse to understand it to be over a sexual matter is indicated by his giving another account of the same incident shortly after in which his father appears as King David. The Biblical allusion is clear. This second version, entitled "Solomon's Dream" and appearing in *Stages On Life's Way* (1845), explains how Solomon, coming upon David groaning in spiritual despair, later dreams that the king is punished by God by being given wealth and position at the price of having to hug to himself the knowledge of God's wrath.

This must have been Michael Pedersen Kierkegaard's view of his own rise from poverty to wealth also, when, though strong and well, he retired from business at the unusually early age of forty to spend his days in study and meditation. But there was an even darker side yet to the supposition that his prosperity was a punishment. His first wife had died childless. One of the children of his second marriage died in 1819, and another in 1822. Then, from 1832 to 1835 the old man, in his late seventies, lost three more children and their mother also. Only Søren and his older brother Peter Christian were left; and death had claimed their five brothers and sisters before they were thirty-four—that is, none had lived beyond the age of Christ. To be condemned to linger on while his family were taken one by one: that was a penalty indicating that he was no ordinary sinner, and that he must have committed the sin against the Holy Ghost, the unforgivable sin.

His father's understanding of the literal shadow of death that lay over them all must have impressed itself on Søren about this time, as is shown in the following entry in the *Journals,* written in 1838:

Then it was that the great earthquake occurred, the terrible revolution which suddenly forced upon me a new and infallible law of interpretation of all the facts. Then I suspected that my father's great age was not a divine blessing but rather a curse; that the outstanding intellectual gifts of our family were only given to us in order that we should rend each other to pieces: then I felt the stillness of death grow around me when I saw in my father, an unhappy man who was to outlive us all, a cross on the tomb of all his hopes. There must be a guilt upon the whole family, the punishment of God must be on it; it was to disappear, wiped out by the powerful hand of God, obliterated like an unsuccessful attempt, and only at times did I find a little alleviation in the thought that my father had been allotted the heavy task of calming us with the consolation of religion, ministering to us so that a better world should be open to us even though we were overtaken by the punishment which the Jews always called down upon their enemies: that all recollection of us should be utterly wiped out, that we should no longer be found (Dru, 243).

The specific sin weighing on his father's conscience is described in another journal entry, written by Søren in 1846:

How terrible about the man who once as a little boy, while herding the flocks on the heaths of Jutland, suffering greatly, in hunger and in want, stood upon a hill and cursed God—and the man was unable to forget it even when he was eighty-two years old (Dru, 556).

Michael Pedersen Kierkegaard was eighty-two in 1838. That year his youngest son was twenty-five and thus, in Danish law, an adult. It may well have been relief over learning at this time the full narrative of his father's long-concealed secret that enabled Søren to write in the *Journals* of his feelings at the initial impact of the "earthquake," when he knew the effect but not the cause of the "curse" upon his family.

Such, at any rate, was the root of the "silent despair" which engulfed the elder Kierkegaard and was communicated so indirectly and yet so powerfully to his children. Eight years after Søren's death, H. P. Barfod, the first editor of his manuscripts, showed the 1846 entry in the *Journals* quoted above to Peter Christian, who was then Bishop of Aalborg. Bishop Peter broke down and cried, exclaiming, "This is my father's story—and ours too." And he explained to Barfod that his father had indeed regarded his boyhood outburst as the sin against the Holy Ghost.

Nevertheless, the punishment Michael Pedersen Kierkegaard believed himself to have incurred was not laid upon him, for he died in 1838, a few months after making his confession. Søren survived him by seventeen years, Peter by fifty.

It has been necessary to give in some detail this particular strand in Kierkegaard's family history. Thus isolated it tends to throw the tragic—or, if you will, the morbid—element into too stark relief. There is another and much brighter side of his experience which has yet to be noted. Nevertheless, without allowing the dark side to appear in its full intensity we cannot see his life's work in perspective. How we estimate both his genius and his limitations depends, rather precisely, upon how we react to the strange and tangled pattern of the relationship between father and son, with all its tensions of aloofness and intimacy, terror and confidence, sternness and compassion, pain and love. Certainly, Kierkegaard's mission as an exponent of Christianity found its focus in the lesson he learned from his father concerning the centrality in human existence of guilt and forgiveness.

From one point of view, the view regarding Kierkegaard's religious upbringing as a major factor in a "case history," we seem to have here a documented confirmation of the truth of Sigmund Freud's analysis of religion. It could be laid on the line as follows.

According to Freud, religion is an illusion perpetuated by man's psychological dependence upon the father image. When Kierkegaard records in his *Journals*, "I have, quite literally, lived with God as one lives with one's father" (Dru, 771), it is not hard to think that perhaps he did not press home his insight literally enough. There are passages to be found in his writings where the distinction between Kierkegaard's God and Kierkegaard's father, and between pleasing the one and pleasing the other, seem virtually to disappear. Freud's explanation that all father figures represent society and its demands is supported by Kierkegaard's identifying his father with what he called "the Rule," i.e., the inculcation of a sense of duty in the child. And Freud's theory that the external commands of society, becoming internalized, build up

student of theology which he had been told to be, still obediently learning his lessons and turning in his assignments, endlessly and tirelessly. The demon driving him to his authorship was his father's voice within him.

Yet every slave must rebel somehow against the tyranny denying him the right to freedom, and Kierkegaard was no exception. Unable to confront the authority of his father directly, he found an indirect way through his father's old friend and spiritual adviser, Bishop Mynster. It was Mynster who had confirmed young Søren. Kierkegaard had lost nerve at the point where he had been given the opportunity to repudiate his father's right to be the sole interpreter of him of the Rule. He had not had the firmness required to admit that he himself had been reared on lies, that the Rule he had been bound to was spurious, or that the wisdom he had revered was folly.

But increasingly he came to think that the Christianity he had accepted unquestioningly from his father was questionable in Mynster, in spite of the fact that Mynster, the leader of believers, was the living link with the dead believer Michael Pedersen Kierkegaard—or perhaps because of it. Since Mynster became the primate of the Danish State Church, revered in the official Christian community much as his father had been revered in his family community, Kierkegaard began to single him out as his special adversary. He distinguished sharply between genuine Christianity, the product of his father's teaching in himself, and spurious or hypocritical Christianity, as taught by the Lutheran establishment headed by Mynster. Still inhibited by the memory of Mynster's closeness to his father, he did not openly attack the rule of Christianity which he named "Christendom" until after the primate's death. But at that moment, he abandoned his authorship for what he thought of as action. In a series of pamphlets he then began with the utmost bitterness to denounce the established Church as *the* enemy which must be destroyed in the name of truth and righteousness.

What is so remarkable about Kierkegaard's attack upon religious officialdom—which, after all, can be paralleled in general by the angry protests of nearly every religious reformer in recorded history—is that it lacked all reforming zeal. Kierkegaard did not call for a purer religion in Denmark, though he denied in general the compatibility between Christianity and a State Church. He demanded, specifically, a statement on the part of the Church that it was not what it had claimed to be, that it did not represent true Christianity. He asked, in effect, that Mynster's spiritual heirs should apologize on their departed leader's behalf for the Primate's personal duplicity, that they should dissociate themselves from this father figure who had stood beside his own father, and that the apology should be made to him because he felt entitled to a fully public admission of guilt on the part of those who had made him suffer privately. Closely associated with his conviction that the established Church could cleanse itself only through such a public confession was his shrill complaint that his country had failed to appreciate the exceptional genius in its midst, to buy his books, to understand his message, and to listen to his scoldings with contrition instead of scorn. At the same time, he looked upon his "rejection" as proof that he was a true imitator of his Master, who, himself forsaken by the fickle multitude and misunderstood by his own followers, promised his disciples unpopularity, persecution, and death.

The "action" of his pamphleteering attack on the Church no doubt precipitated his death, since it exhausted his small reserves of strength. Collapsing on the streets of Copenhagen on October 2, 1855, he was taken to a hospital and died the next month. But if it was a sacrificial death, it was so only because he gave himself up to irreconcilable forces within himself: love and hatred of his father, the man he believed had died for him and the man who had actually deprived him of all joy in the world of the living. Toward the end of his *Journals* (which he discontinued in December 1854) he thanks God first of all for the fact "that no living being owes its existence to me" (Dru, 1400). When the thought of fatherhood had become so repellent, how could he claim still to love the Father? There was no way, in life. . . .

Looked at from a purely external viewpoint, Kierkegaard's career was just such a contradiction as has been outlined, a contradiction destined to end, as it did, in some form of self-destruction. If this were the only possible viewpoint, then we would simply turn away in pity, or else keep the story in mind as a warning and a horrid example.

Ironically enough, Kierkegaard's name has in fact gone down in the history of his homeland as a horrid example—on one level, that is. The name Søren, once almost the most common boy's name in Denmark, has become disused because of the popular use of the phrase "Don't be a Søren!" That phrase is a legacy from the times when Kierkegaard was made into a figure of fun by the caricatures of him in *The Corsair*. Of course, on a different level, Kierkegaard's name recalls to his countrymen the memory of one of their greatest writers, and probably the most brilliant stylist ever to handle their language. Perhaps there is a parable here, suggesting that it is unwise of us to base our total estimate of a man on a caricature of him. And a caricature is what results when we adopt only one set of criteria for assessing a fellow human being.

Nevertheless, in some respects, a caricature is actually better and nearer life than a portrait. And, though the sketch presented over the past few pages is oversimplified to the point of grotesque falsification, it also is much more than a lie. It points to facts that have to be met in any honest assessment of Kierkegaard's authorship and its relevance for today.

There is an argument favored by some Kierkegaard admirers to the effect that the morbid aspects of this genius do not matter, because he himself knew and analyzed his morbidity better than any one else had done since.[2] But this will not do. Kierkegaard was nobody's fool, and he turned on himself the same penetrating intellectual curiosity he used to probe the world round about him. He knew that there was a sickness in him, that the "melancholy" he had been steeped in since early childhood affected his estimate of the universe and at times seriously distorted his judgment. He could never have guessed the exact measure of his limitations, though, or have been aware of the drives within him leading (for example) to the unleashing of his unconscious hostilities upon Bishop Mynster.[3] To expect anything of the kind would be to expect the impossible of any inhabitant of this planet, and certainly of this particular one.

What Kierkegaard did and did well, on the other hand, was to insist—as he does in *Fear and Trembling*—that there is truth in the old tag about genius and madness being closely allied, so long as we have sense to see that the genius is a genius because, in spite of everything, he keeps his sanity (F.A.T., 116). It is not the narrowness of the margin but the brilliant exploitation of what lies within it that counts. We should beware, when a man admits he is sometimes crazy, lest we imagine he is also stupid, and, thinking to patronize him, receive much more than we bargained for.

In 1846, Kierkegaard wrote in his *Journals*:

> *This is how I have understood myself in my entire literary work.* I am in the profoundest sense an unhappy individuality which from its earliest years has been nailed fast to some suffering or other, bordering upon madness, and which must have its deeper roots in a disproportion between soul and body; for (and that is what is extraordinary) it has no relation to my mind. On the contrary, perhaps because of the strained relation between soul and body my mind has received a tensile strength that is rare (Dru, 600).

His toughness of mind, he went on to say, never enabled him to throw off his melancholy, but it enabled him to bear it. His brother Peter seems to have lacked this resource. In his old age he hugged to himself the same phantasy of having committed the unforgivable sin which his father had entertained and was forced to retire from his duties, while his son actually became insane. Kierkegaard mentioned in 1848 that one of the crosses he had to bear was Peter's becoming "morbidly religious" (Dru, 841). Even Søren's final onslaught on the established Church, with all its overtones of desperation, is often funny as well as savage. And the consistency of thought which runs through his whole authorship until the pamphleteering period is that of a questing intelligence, not the rigid pseudologicality of monomania.

This is where we need to keep in mind that other legacy from his childhood which, equally with the motif of melancholy, helped to make him what he was. When Kierkegaard adapts the "silent despair" story from the *Journals* for inclusion in *Stages on Life's Way* he adds (192), "However, they rarely regarded one another in this way, for their daily intercourse was characterized by the cheerfulness of gay and lively conversation." Michael Pedersen Kierkegaard's habit of taking Søren round the living room on imaginary walks through the town, instead of allowing him to walk out of doors, is frequently mentioned as part of the child's "crazy" upbringing. Perhaps it was, yet it was a high delight to them both, and for Søren one of the reminders that he was the old man's "Benjamin," the specially regarded son who in consequence drew Peter's resentment. From his father's concretely focused imagination Søren received the inspiration that was to make him take to literature as a duck to water, and from him too he learned the power of reason directed by a discriminating mind. Soon he was allowed to listen to the debates that took place in the merchant's home, where his father would listen in silence while a visitor built up a case, was asked whether he had anything to add, and then found the structure promptly demolished by a superior analytical mind. The human quality of the intelligence, as well as the divine authority of Christianity, was impressed upon him in those years. The lesson stuck.

We continue to listen to Kierkegaard, not because he provides us with an intriguing case history of a morbid personality, but because he seems to have something to say to us that we do not find elsewhere. Moreover, he shames us, whenever we feel inclined to reject his conclusions out of hand, by flashing before us a rigor of mind that shows up the flabbiness of our customary ways of thinking. He decidely will not be patronized. And, when we are inclined to excuse ourselves by saying that this is all intellectual legerdemain, and that there is a big flaw somewhere that vitiates his whole argument, then he challenges us to put our finger on the precise place where he goes wrong. And this is not so easy, because, if we find one spot where we think we can wriggle out of his logic, then he has twenty other propositions ready waiting for us and asking us if we really wish to test our skill against his.

And his challenge to us is never on the basis of a simple call to match wit against wit, either. He asks us to share a vision which he has, to probe the foundations of the convictions we take for granted, and to look again at prejudices which we have too easily taken to be self-evident truths. He throws in our way stories as well as argumentation. This insatiable prodder of mental laziness—this *fork*—actually has the gall to assume that we shall not just learn from him but also learn with him.

So, once we have been brought up against Kierkegaard's sheer intellectual energy and suppleness in debate, it is difficult to maintain the theory that his separation of philosophy from religion, for example, is to be explained in easy terms as the *idée fixe* of the neurotic. And the same holds all along the line. Deluded in some respects and to some degree he may have been. Yet, beyond any maybe, he was more serious than most of us can claim to be about the need for us to strip off our masks and learn to live with our own faces in the real world lying beyond our pasteboard make-believe.

In order to do justice to the unnervingly complex and fascinating mystery we call reality, Kierkegaard developed an intellectual way of approach to it that he thought to be an indispensable tool for the thinking man. More accurately, he adopted it from previous thinkers, and then adapted it for his own use. This was the way of *dialectic*, the method of argument balancing every Yes against a No, the method which Plato learned from Socrates and elaborated for the purposes of his own philosophy. Kierkegaard did not consider the means we took, when we sought the truth about reality, to be a casual matter. Just as there were appropriate ways of addressing different people if we wanted to get a reply from them, so with our approach to the universe around us. For himself, Kierkegaard believed the universe found its final explanation in the infinitely extended light streaming from the single point of the love of God. But how could that light be reflected in our minds? Dialectic, he urged, was the prism that could bend the light to bring it straight to us.

II
The Strategy
of the Dialectic

STARTING FROM Kierkegaard's early introduction to the exciting intricacies of debate through listening to his father taking on all comers and worsting them fairly through superior dialectical skill, we can easily understand how later in life he placed so much importance in dialectic, the play of Yes against No. More than that, there is here a very important clue to the complex, not to say tortuous, course of his authorship.

To begin with, he was exposed to intellectual activity being carried on in a real-life situation—or, as he was to teach us all to say, "existentially." The object of the debates at which he was present was to discover the rights and wrongs of some matter. That is to say, its aim was "objective truth." But he saw that the conclusion was not arrived at immediately; it had to be worked out. (As a mature thinker he put this simple observation into technical terms by speaking of all knowledge as "mediation," and of the act of aiming at acquiring knowledge as "reflection.") The human possibility of embarking upon the quest for knowledge appeared to him always as a marvelous thing, far too important to be considered in any such general term as "the power of reason." For what was involved was always someone, an individual person, engaged in relating himself to the truth.

Second, he saw that, although an argument often ended with one of the parties to it being victorious, this was not in the least a proof that the purpose intended by the clash of wits had been achieved. He guessed that his father could have

[27]

started just as easily at his opponent's position, inverted his arguments, and still have carried the day. Possessing superior dialectical skill from the ability to follow a chain of thought through to a foreseen conclusion was very different from relating oneself to the truth. From this insight he developed the very important concepts which he was to call "objective uncertainty" and "subjectivity." In the event of there being no way of demonstrating who was right and who was wrong (which happened invariably wherever more than verifiable "matters of fact" were involved), the outcome of any debate was necessarily settled by "passion" or determined conviction. One party just gave way when he could see no purpose in trying to carry on. His "passion" had grown cold, at least for the moment. However, as the seventeenth-century satirist Samuel Butler remarked, "He that complies against his will/Is of his own opinion still." That man probably goes home determined to think up better arguments for the next encounter. And human beings are bound to make up their minds "passionately" in most of the concrete concerns of their existence. They have to choose, rightly or wrongly, and stand to take the consequences.

Third, Kierkegaard never for one moment imagined that our decisions, however passionate, justified themselves. It is astonishing to find how widespread even now is the notion that his stand on "subjectivity" meant he thought every man must reject solutions other men have worked out for life's problems, but must insist upon making his own choices in his own way. The principle of what's-right-for-me's-not-right-for-you-for-you're-not-me was the last one Kierkegaard would ever have agreed to, since his whole authorship was dedicated to advancing the very opposite. In brief, whatever else he said, he said very clearly that Christianity was for everybody, and that Christianity was not what people thought it might be but was what it was and always had been. The task of his authorship, then, was not to commend Christianity to anyone—for why should *opinion* matter in this connection?—but to show what it was in its own right and what claims it made. That being done, it was up to his reader to decide what he was to do about it, to choose, in fact, between life and death as Moses asked Israel to choose at Sinai beside the mountain of God.

The goal to be reached, so Kierkegaard maintained, was not in doubt. It was to relate oneself to the truth. And the method of reaching the goal was not in doubt, either. It was to decide correctly, to make a choice. But the problem at this point presented itself in its full seriousness. How was the individual to decide? Upon what basis could he proceed to a wise choice instead of a foolish one, find life instead of death? Now it became imperative to discover whether the truth presented itself in any way that would make it possible for an individual to grasp hold of a clue to its proper nature. If we are to relate ourselves to anything, then we must know, at least, what it is that we are related to if and when we establish that relationship. Otherwise universal skepticism will reign. And we must know that the possibility of establishing such a relationship is a possibility for us. Otherwise we will accept one or other of the choices open to the skeptic: despair, indifference, or blindly egotistical self-assertion—which are at bottom one and the same. Kierkegaard believed that the truth did not remain opaque to us, but that, in fact, it had made itself accessible to us—in Christianity. Its nature was not unknowable. On the contrary, since it was revealed to the individual who related himself to it in his existence, it was a fit subject for reflection. Since Christianity was the truth actually present in existence, we could not know it to be true except by relating ourselves to it in actuality, in existence. Yet, that being so, there was no contradiction in putting the truth of Christianity in intellectual terms. Only now existence was not encountered as such, of course, but solely in reflection. Therefore the form in which the reflecting mind would have to state its conclusion would be as a possibility, not as an actuality. The form it would take would be: *if* Christianity is the truth, *then* it must be lived and not approached in abstraction from existence.

It is of the utmost importance to realize that Kierkegaard's "authorship" began only after he had become completely convinced that Christianity was the truth. Neglect of this fact makes nonsense of the authorship and leads to an entirely mistaken view of the "dialectic" he employed throughout his writings. He insisted, indeed, that he had always been a Christian. But it seems clear that in the period preceding and— especially—following "the great earthquake" he was at any rate detached enough from the faith in which he had been reared to consider that it might be an illusion and therefore a means of leading men away from their proper existence instead of showing them how life should be lived. What he never abandoned was the sense of the responsibility of the individual for fulfilling his personal calling under God, a sense born of the severity of his upbringing in his father's house, where he was made to understand that each hour was a call to duty, and that the whole of life lay open to decisions affecting one's eternal destiny.

An early expression of his outlook in this regard is recorded in 1835, when he wrote:

> What I really lack is to be clear in my mind what I am to do, not what I am to know, except in so far as a certain understanding must precede action. The thing is to understand myself, to see what God really wishes *me* to do; the thing is to find a truth which is true for *me*, to find *the idea for which I can live and die*. . . . I certainly do not deny that I still recognize an *imperative of understanding* and that through it one can work upon men, *but it must be taken up into my life*, and *that is* what I now recognize as the most important thing (Dru, 22).

Three years later he was writing, with a sense of determination:

> I mean to labour to achieve a far more inward relation to Christianity; hitherto I have fought for its truth while in a sense standing outside it. In a purely outward sense I have carried Christ's cross, like Simon of Cyrene (Dru, 211).

In 1840, during the course of his pilgrimage to his father's birthplace in Jutland, he mused upon the task awaiting him and of his debt to his father:

[30]

I learnt from him the meaning of fatherly love and so was given some idea of divine fatherly love, the one unshakable thing in life, the true archimedean point (Dru, 335).

His search for an idea for which he could live and die was over; though the way in which he was to fight for the truth of Christianity was not as yet clear to him. It required the :olt of his break with Regine to bring him to the realization that his task was to be to respond to the imperative of understanding and, through it, to work upon men. When he had put behind him the thought of marriage and a normal career involved in the responsibilities of family life, he produced the first book of his authorship. He wrote it under a pseudonym: Victor Eremita—Victor (the victorious one) the Hermit. The choice of this name shows that he was conscious of knowing something in his own experience of the victory of Christian faith that has overcome the world (1 John 5:4), and also that he was certain his own Christian vocation meant a voluntary commitment to celibacy. The name of the book was *Either/Or*.

When his authorship was well advanced Kierkegaard wrote an explanation of it called *The Point of View for My Work as an Author*. In it he explained why he had chosen to bring out a whole series of works attributed to various imaginary personages. The reason he gave was that he had meant to deceive. If any one objects that deception is an ugly thing, Kierkegaard comments, he "betrays the fact that he is not over-well versed in dialectics" since this is the only way of bringing into the truth a person who is in an illusion.

What then does it mean, 'to deceive'? It means that one does not begin *directly* with the matter one wants to communicate, but begins by accepting the other man's illusion as good money. So (to stick to the theme with which this work especially deals) one does not begin thus: I am a Christian; you are not a Christian. . . . The deception consists in the fact that one talks thus merely to get to the religious theme (P.O.V., 40-41).

Now we know from statements made elsewhere that *Either/*

Or and the two pseudonymous works following it, *Repetition* and *Fear and Trembling* (published simultaneously), were written for Regine, explaining obliquely his reasons for breaking the engagement and holding out the hope that there might yet be a reconciliation. Given the devious and mystification-loving character of his mind, we may well wonder whether Kierkegaard was not supplying in *The Point of View* an explanation made up after the event in order to conceal a change in plan made necessary by Regine's early engagement to another suitor (Fritz Schlegel) and her subsequent marriage. However plausible such a theory may be, the account in *The Point of View* is backed up by the fact that each "literary" book was accompanied from the first by a "religious" one, a lay sermon—or "Edifying Discourse," as he chose to name it. This, an essential part of the scheme, was thus no afterthought.

Kierkegaard's mind *was* devious, yet incapable of downright duplicity. We need not doubt that his whole authorship was planned carefully from the start. The plan, after all, was open and supple enough to permit development in any particular direction required by the events of the times. Only the general strategy of the dialectic was decided. Tactics could be varied. Again, quite evidently, the early pseudonymous works are much more than "open letters" to Regine. They *are* ingenious introductions to "the religious theme." Though Kierkegaard may impress us as having rejoiced too much over his elaborate plan of deception, it was a plan that worked. And its development could be justified.

To appreciate Kierkegaard's explanation of the intent in his authorship, we might transpose his argument into terms of the debates carried on in Michael Pedersen Kierkegaard's house. Perhaps the visitor to his home went away crushed by the old gentleman's logic, but inwardly rebelling against his conclusions because they clashed with his own cherished convictions. How could this have been avoided? Surely, only by engaging the emotions ("passions") of the visitor, so that he too felt the excitement ("pathos") of following a chain of reasoning to its end by being caught up in the argument, which seemed to him to be about the concerns which were most real to him.

Kierkegaard was convinced that some such strategy of dialectic was imperative in talking about Christianity in his day. For Denmark was a "Christian" country in a "Christian" civilization—part of "Christendom." Therefore, whenever any talk of Christianity began, people immediately began to think in terms of Christianity as they understood it. And, if it appeared that the person speaking to them had some understanding of Christianity other than their own, they immediately resisted it and were prepared to argue that "real" Christianity was not like that at all. So there was, Kierkegaard observed, a problem in "reflection" involved in "introducing Christianity into Christendom." The idea of Christianity had become so overlaid with "proofs" of the truth of the Christian religion, and with apologetic arguments designed to show that Christianity was the highest and best of religions, that the New Testament foundation of Christianity and the ideals of contemporary European culture had become intertwined until the distance separating the two had become forgotten and their entire compatibility was blandly assumed.

So Kierkegaard proposed to try a new tactic. He would speak, in works assigned to a pseudonymous author, of the things most near to the interests of contemporary man. But in the course of these works, having engaged the attention and sympathy of the reader, he would steer the argument around to topics relating to New Testament Christianity. Of course, the reader might see what was happening somewhere along the line and turn in resentment against the author. But then, Kierkegaard thought, he had at least persuaded the aggrieved reader to "take notice." The reader would have gone with his guide part of the way. He would not have closed his mind from the first, refusing even to consider the propositions being put to him. And the possibility remained that he might take seriously an author who had shown himself able to talk his language and share his interests.

In connection with his program of literary deception Kierkegaard appealed to the example of Socrates. He wrote:

> . . . I for my part tranquilly adhere to Socrates. It is true he was not a Christian; that I know, and yet am thoroughly convinced that he has become one. But he was a dialectician, he conceived everything in terms of reflection. And the question which concerns us here is a purely dialectical one, it is the question of the use of reflection in Christendom (P.O.V., 41).

Socrates was Kierkegaard's lifelong hero, and he himself has been described as the Danish Socrates. He wrote for his dissertation for his master's degree (the equivalent of a modern Ph.D.) *The Concept of Irony; with Constant Reference to Socrates.* It was presented in 1841 and was the second book he wrote, the first being *From the Papers of One Still Living,* [1] published in 1838, a critical reaction to Hans Christian Andersen's novel *Only a Fiddler.*

At the time when he wrote *The Concept of Irony* Kierkegaard was to a large extent under the influence of Hegel, who was the dominating intellectual presence in the Denmark of his university days; and in the dissertation he largely agreed with Hegel's opinion that the contribution Socrates made to the thought of his time was a negative one, challenging current dogmatic assumptions rather than suggesting any very positive alternative. Quite soon, Kierkegaard altered his estimate of Socrates—though not so violently as he altered his estimate of Hegel. Socrates became for him the highest example of the reflective thinker who taught the creative function of doubt without being a doubter. As he saw it, Socrates kept to the fore, against all purely speculative thinking, the duty of the thinker to see things as they were, however humdrum or mundane they might seem to be. At the same time, Socrates was firm in his belief that man's existence pointed to an absolute world of values, which were concretely present to him in ethical demands. Man was to live in the here and now, yet always viewing it in the light of the infinite.

For Kierkegaard the reason why Socrates escaped the error

of abstract, generalizing thinking was that he respected the "given" in human existence, including his own individuality and the personal claims made upon him by his specific situation as an Athenian citizen, and so was able to live his philosophy. "The majority of men are curtailed 'I's,'"wrote Kierkegaard (Dru, 1376). "What was planned by nature as a possibility capable of being sharpened into an I is soon dulled into a third person." But Socrates, Kierkegaard continued, was not a third person in the sense that he avoided going into danger or staking his life; he was an "I." An "I" cannot avoid the "pathos" of existence, but embraces it to the end. Not only did Socrates stand as a true "I" against the contemporary Sophists, who taught a bogus wisdom because their teaching was at odds with their lives, but his dialectical strategy was adapted to his situation. While others claimed to know, he claimed only to be ignorant and desirous of receiving enlightenment from those about him. The strategy produced results by making his hearers think for themselves under the stimulus of his questions. As Socrates himself said, he became a midwife assisting at the birth of wisdom in others.

Socrates' dialectical midwifery inspired Kierkegaard to imitate his "maieutic art" through what he terms the "indirect communication" of the pseudonymous works. Allied with this approach went another one, which was indeed its complement and logical conclusion: silence. Kierkegaard once observed:

> 'There is a time for silence.' That may be learnt from the highest example: He was silent. I have learnt it from a lesser one, for Socrates had it in his power to save his life—by flattering the people (Dru, 765).

That he had been concerned with the importance of timely silence is indicated by the pseudonym Johannes de Silentio (John out of the Silence) he attached to *Fear and Trembling*.

What was said of Carlyle, that he was the prophet of silence in forty volumes, might be thought to apply to Kierkegaard also. The recommendation to silence seems to accord badly with the torrent of words that flowed so rapidly from his pen. Once again, Kierkegaard is not to be refuted by a simple jibe. We shall have to get up very early in the morning if we wish to catch him napping. The point of his use of dialectic is that truth is not to be laid bare by an easy appeal to "facts"—since the point of the pursuit of truth is to discover what the human facts really are! He wrote: "Every truth is nevertheless truth only to a certain degree; when it goes beyond, the counterpoint appears, and it becomes untruth" (Hong, 753).

Of course Kierkegaard wrote a lot. He had a lot to say, and he has never lacked a reader. He knew he would become a celebrity, though he shuddered at the thought of having "a public." But he believed that the modern age, like that of Socrates, was obsessed by the wish to be entertained, and above all to be entertained by *twaddle*—which meant chiefly current half-truths and popular prejudices in the public mind being dressed up with a show of profundity or superficial wit. And he thought that there were unpopular ideas that might be also put entertainingly; even though, once the idea had got through to the reader, he might find something very different from entertainment. Any one can pick up in an odd moment a book with the title *Fear and Trembling*. He may actually become engrossed in it, if he finds it well-written, and the thoughts in it striking and novel. But what if it leads him actually to experience, for just one moment, fear and trembling? To fear and tremble is obviously, in our accepted way of thinking, something unpleasant if not peculiarly disgusting and indicative of morbidity and psychological unbalance. Kierkegaard felt that his use of the dialectical strategy of indirect communication might, just possibly, help his reader to question the assumptions he held in common with those around him; that it might be maieutic teaching of the kind that Socrates had used to help his contemporaries in a similar situation.

To all this the objection may be urged that Kierkegaard's methods, even if we grant his good faith, represent a *reductio ad absurdum* of religious apologetic. In saying that he stands with Socrates against the Sophists he has succeeded in tying himself in a tangle of sophistries. When one comes to the point of having to commend silence by indulging in a diarrhea of words, or of explaining New Testament Christianity through involved arguments requiring a plethora of terms borrowed from the obscurer reaches of philosophical history, then it is time to call a halt and return to plain words with plain meanings. Isn't this what is wrong with religious writers, past and present, that they do not address the world in terms that can be understood or that give practical guidance in solving present-day problems?

Kierkegaard's answer, in effect, is that Christian belief is very simple. Living this belief is hard, because its simplicity is shattering to all who lack the simple integrity of purity of heart; and that means all of us. It is we who are unwilling to enter the narrow way of simplicity. We are masters in the art of avoiding our plain duty of disguising the starkness of our situation before God. We are disobedient sons who manufacture a thousand excuses for not carrying out the Father's command. The same voice that complains one minute that Christian teaching is so complex and laden with abstruse terms that it cannot be understood, the next minute is objecting that it is so naive and childish it may have suited the days when people simply believed what they were told because they were uneducated and superstitious, but is unbelievable now that we think for ourselves and know something about the real nature of the universe.

The consensus of a sophisticated age, in short, is that simple faith is for the simple-minded, not for us who are most incensed by being thought simple.

This was the situation Kierkegaard faced. Faith, he believed, was simplicity itself. It disclosed itself to us in a flash of instant recognition not requiring reflection—what he termed "immediacy." But faith for man, as a thinking being, must always be *immediacy after reflection.* Note that he did not believe this order was something which the early Christians had not known, but which we, the true sophisticates, demanded. This was the universal condition for man, the being who possesses self-consciousness as the gift of his created existence. What happens is that the *content* of reflection changes with the changing horizons of human culture. We do not always approach faith with the same preconceptions in our mind.

We would be flattering ourselves to imagine that our horizons are so very much larger than those of men in earlier ages that our reflection is of a range and penetration surpassing anything that has been experienced before. Kierkegaard could see no evidence for such an assumption. Knowledge about man in his existence had no necessary connection with knowledge about the world of things and our power to control the environment. Rather, the opposite was true. Thus Socrates the pagan showed himself to have a greater awareness of the questions we ought to put to ourselves about our nature and our destiny than most present-day philosophers in Christendom after two thousand years of Christian history. The fact that we had a long "historical perspective" to aid us did not count for much, since we were not asking the right questions which would enable us to find the answers we needed. For those answers, the perspective of a single human life was long enough. If we could not use that to learn our lesson, adding an infinite quantity would make no qualitative difference.

Kierkegaard was made aware of the contemporary myopia in reading the human problem through observing the reception given by his contemporaries to two impressive cultural events: the romantic movement and the philosophy of Hegel. Like every other educated person of his times, he himself was influenced—"influenced" is really too inadequate a word—by both. Upon reflection he rejected both, though he could not have shaken them off entirely, of course, even had he wished to. Romanticism was not a single, definable doctrine. He contented himself with pointing out its dangers when used to form a generalized philosophy of life. Hegel's teaching was specific, though wide-ranging. In combating "the [Hegelian] System" throughout his authorship (once *The Concept of Irony* was behind him), Kierkegaard was sure he was doing much more than finding holes in the argument of an able thinker with whose conclusions he disagreed. Rather, he felt himself to be opposing a technique of reflection which the brilliance of Hegel's constructive powers had succeeded in making universal for a whole age. In a sense, Hegel's genius had mainly given a new solidity to a trend in modern man's approach to reality that had begun with Descartes, an approach which tried to encompass all things through trust in the omnicompetence of the human power of thought. But in Hegel thought had reached a new level of self-confidence. It believed that, for all practical purposes, it had come to comprehend God entirely, and so to displace him.

The Hegelian dialectic thus came to represent for Kierkegaard the antithesis of the Socratic dialectic and the supreme obstacle in the way of the reception of the Christian faith by the modern world. The reason for his taking Hegel so seriously as a threat to Christianity was that Hegelian logic, through its principle of "mediation," encouraged the belief that it was possible—and necessary—to look for the meaning of life in world history instead of in the will of God for the individual. Since Hegelian philosophy asserted the identity of the rational and the real, it claimed to understand everything rationally, *including Christianity*. There were no irreconcilable contradictions which could not be overcome through the principle of mediation, and so no mystery which it could not explain, *including the inner life of God*. It followed that the Christian claim for the primacy of the life of faith was disallowed in the name of higher principle. Under such a dispensation the "pathos" of life was banished along with its contradictions; and, although this was done ostensibly in the interests of freeing the human consciousness, the result was an immense impoverishment of man's ability to see the world in its full wonder, beauty, and terror. Where Christianity had called man to find the abundant life through the gift of faith that enabled man to love what was infinitely beyond him, the principle of mediation invited him to understand everything life could offer without having to do more than think about it. People had been persuaded to consent to being robbed of their existence by being offered the painless knowledge of good and evil. They were being beguiled, a second time, with the promise that lost them Eden in the beginning.[2]

Kierkegaard's authorship became, in consequence, oriented to a large extent to the contemporary mind that had become drunk on the heady wine of Hegelianism. To a very large extent the terminology he used was Hegelian, though, of course, worn with a difference. In place of Biblical terminology he used either Hegel's phrases or others conceived in direct opposition to them. It was not accidental that the first work of this authorship, *Either/Or,* directly confronted the principle of mediation. It countered the basis of the System at its central point, and did so by insisting on Kierkegaard's own dialectic of confrontation and choice. But, throughout, Kierkegaard sought to place in front of his reader the Christian call to choose life in the decision of faith by insisting upon the categories of existence and subjectivity in contradiction to those of speculation and (philosophical) "science." In order to upset his contemporaries' trust in the philosophical outlook which had been accepted as the lastest advance in enlightenment, elevating their generation above the times of ignorance and superstition, he told them that this view of life was one which could not be taken seriously; it was merely comic. Assuming it could explain the universe, it did not find room for the most commonplace events in everyday life—a sneeze, for instance.

Mistaking abstraction for reality is the burden of the accusation which Kierkegaard leveled against Hegel. He wrote:

> If Hegel had written the whole of his logic and then said, in the preface, that it was merely an experiment in thought in which he had even begged the question in many places, then he would certainly have been the greatest thinker who had ever lived. As it is he is merely comic (Dru, 497).

But he knew, too, that it was not enough to try to laugh Hegelianism out of men's minds. Once this way of reflection had become part of the outlook of an age, it had to be replaced by another that made contact with it and indirectly subverted it—thus his use of quasi-Hegelian terminology. In his various pseudonymous books he returned to different aspects of the theme of the challenge of existence for the individual as over against the loss of this challenge in the System. His philosophical attack came to a head when he countered Hegel's Reason with the Absolute Paradox. Only after that did he approach direct "reflection" (the word is one of his Hegelian borrowings) upon the meaning of Christianity.

How rightly he judged the force of the Hegelian vision to dazzle men and bewitch their reflective capacities is something I shall have more to say about when looking at how Kierkegaard himself has been "used" by twentieth-century philosophers. But now it is time to look more closely at the alternative way of reflection he elaborated in his authorship.

III

Reflection on Existence

SO FAR IN THIS STUDY I have dealt with the "how" of Kierkegaard—how he came to be a writer on Christianity, how he used the dialectical method, and so forth—rather than with the content of his teaching, the "what." There is an interesting item in the *Journals* showing that Kierkegaard himself made a good deal of the distinction between the "how" and the "what." It comes where he is commenting on a piece of the argument set forth in his book the *Concluding Unscientific Postscript,* written under his pseudonym Johannes Climacus, John the Climber (to whom is also attributed the *Philosophical Fragments):*

> In all that is usually said about Johannes Climacus being purely subjective and so on, people have forgotten, in addition to everything concrete about him, that in one of the last sections he shows that the curious thing is: that there is a 'how' which has this quality, that if *it* is truly given, then the 'what' is also given; and that is the 'how' of faith. Here, quite certainly, we have inwardness at its maximum proving to be objectivity once again. And this is an aspect of the principle of subjectivity which, so far as I know, has never before been presented or worked out (Dru, 1021).

But now, in seeming defiance of his wishes, I find it necessary to turn briefly to look at the "what" of faith as Kierkegaard presented it. In thus putting asunder the pair he joined together, I do not think that violence is being done to his intention. For he was speaking about the route we must follow to find the reality of faith as such, not about the place we can occupy to get a reasonably good idea of what he took to be faith. More of that later, though. For the minute it is enough to recognize that, unless we have some notion of the meaning he put into such terms as "subjectivity" and "inwardness," we shall not make much sense of his argument for the validity of putting the "how" of faith before the "what" and making the former include the latter.

To attempt to summarize here the contents of the books comprising the authorship would certainly result in losing the forest behind the trees. Besides, there is no lack of guidance in this area, but rather an *embarras de richesses*. [1] It might be thought, perhaps, that the *Edifying Discourses* accompanying the "literary" works would provide a door opening into the "what" of his teaching, especially since in *The Point of View* he wrote of the beginning of his authorship in 1843:

> I held out *Either/Or* to the world in my left hand, and in my right the *Two Edifying Discourses*; but all, or as good as all, grasped with their right what I held in my left (**P.O.V.**, 20).

However, he was referring then to the public's obtuseness in ignoring a manifestly religious book and preferring one not obviously to do with Christianity. All that this tells us is that he would have liked to have been accepted as a religious author; not that the *Edifying Discourses*, then or later, contained any special key to his thinking. There is really no short cut to that. And it remains true that the shape of his thought is most readily grasped by us—as it seems to have come to consciousness in him—through the process of his opposition to the Hegelian philosophy.

The very titles of some of the most important of his books exhibit this opposition. *Either/Or* challenged Hegel's principle of mediation; *Philosophical Fragments; or A Fragment of Philosophy* jokingly indicated his rejection of Hegel's System; *Concluding Unscientific Postscript to the Philosophical Fragments* mocked Hegel's belief that with the publication of his *Logic* had come "the elevation of philosophy to the position of science." Other works showed the same thing indirectly. *Stages On Life's Way* was a Kierkegaardian equivalent (inner, personal history) to the Hegelian preoccupation with world history; *Fear and Trembling* and *The Concept of Dread* were comparisons-by-contrast with Hegel's concept of "Spirit certain-of-itself." We do not have to imagine that Kierkegaard, so to speak, always sat with Hegel's portrait on the desk and looked at it before writing on any and every topic. But we need to remember, equally, how aware he was that the intellectual climate of his century was being formed by the propagation of ideas contradicting his most basic convictions, yet, so it appeared, irresistibly attractive to the age. It was inevitable that his choice of topics and his manner of treating these should alike reflect—deliberately or otherwise—his wish to loosen the stranglehold such ideas had gained on men's minds.

To proclaim Christianity and to turn his reader back from the path along which Hegel had persuaded the public to walk, then, were two aspects of the same task. Carrying out the task was a knotty problem. It could not be done by laying on the line Christian doctrines and pointing out their incongruity with Hegelianism; since plainly there was great enthusiasm all around for the opposite enterprise of demonstrating how the new philosophy supported Christian teaching and made it believable for modern man. Nor was there a way out by appealing to the Church; since churchmen (notably H. L. Martensen, Kierkegaard's onetime tutor at the university and later Mynster's successor) were the leaders of the synthesizing movement.

The dialectical approach indicated indirect communication as the appropriate solution. By starting with the subject which the reader was prepared to find interesting to him, and by using terms with which he was familiar, you led him to accept (or at least to consider) conclusions which he would have rebelled against had he been confronted with them at the first. This meant that Kierkegaard had to be prepared to adopt the kind of terminology which people had learnt from Hegel and his peers. And this is what he did, though increasingly showing his hand. Thus in the *Philosophical Fragments*, though the argument actually is about the possibility of a historical revelation in Christianity, the book sets out to answer, as "a project in thought," the philosophical question posed at its outset: How is it possible for us to know the truth? The name of Christ is never mentioned, and even the name of God is avoided. In keeping with the introduction of Socrates as our guide to solving the problem of truth, the title "the God" is used throughout. However, in the *Concluding Unscientific Postscript* the pseudonymous author Johannes Climacus (he of the *Fragments*) states specifically that his topic is the nature of Christianity. Yet here, too, the problem is stated in philosophical terms with an almost complete absence of a "theological" vocabulary.

The "what" of Christianity as Kierkegaard conceives it, nevertheless, shines through the whole authorship. It is quite obviously conceived by him along the lines of a Chalcedonian orthodoxy (Christ, very God and very Man) with a Lutheran emphasis (faith as trust bestowing complete assurance of salvation through Christ's atoning death and resurrection). However, he had very little interest in theology as such, seldom quoting the great theologians, though he must have read them. He held strongly, too, that Christianity's being conceived *as a doctrine* had resulted in its being completely misunderstood in "Christendom." So we cannot expect to find anything resembling a personal *credo* set out anywhere in his writings, and to try to piece together a compendium of his beliefs from scattered statements would be a misconceived undertaking.

A very interesting suggestion has recently been made in Vernard Eller's *Kierkegaard and Radical Discipleship: A New Perspective.*[2] Comparing Kierkegaard's beliefs (and his attitude toward belief) with those of the German Baptist Brethren ("Dunkers"), Dr. Eller claims that Kierkegaard's Christianity conforms perfectly to the pattern of "classic Protestant sectarianism" that seeks to recover the *practice* of New Testament Christianity by setting up individual commitment to the life of faith in opposition to any church "establishment." There would certainly seem to be many points of contact between the sectarian outlook and Kierkegaard: not only Kierkegaard the antiecclesiastic who came to regard the practice of infant baptism as the chief cause of the loss of Christianity in Christendom, but also Kierkegaard the staunch believer in the authority of the Bible who advised us to read it without a commentary as a love letter from God (Hong, 207, 210) and yet who thought that two entirely different principles operated in the Old and the New Testament (Hong, 206). Dr. Eller's thesis goes far to explain the "unorthodox," i.e., nondoctrinal, slant to Kierkegaard's orthodoxy—for example, why, when holding a Trinitarian view of God, he should discuss the Trinity no more than once and then in the *Journals* (Dru, 1282), not in any of the published works.

But his orthodoxy is there, all right, slant or no. It becomes visible whenever there is some question of modifying traditional belief in the interests of making it acceptable to the ways of thinking of the age. The most explicit statement he makes on this subject is one appearing in part of a long letter to an unidentified confidant, dated Spring 1837. After a freewheeling survey of present tendencies in the cultural scene as these affect politics, literature, and philosophy, Kierkegaard continued:

And now what about Christianity, how has it been dealt with? I entirely agree with your disapproval of the way in which every Christian concept has been so sublimated into a sea of fog that it is impossible to recognize it again. To such concepts as faith, incarnation, tradition, inspiration, which in Christianity must be referred to a particular historical fact, it has seemed good to philosophers to give an entirely different general meaning. . . .(Dru, 88).

It was this process of giving an *entirely different general meaning* to Christian concepts having each an essential relation to *a particular historical fact* that Kierkegaard saw as the cardinal error of Hegel-dominated thinkers supposing themselves to be explaining the "true" meaning of Christian concepts. For Christian concepts arose out of something which

[46]

had happened in history, the sphere of existence. And their purpose was to enable people to reflect upon the meaning of Christianity for their own existence. The movement was from concrete actuality back to concrete actuality.

But to generalize these Christian concepts, to take them out of history in order to relate them to an abstract world history, was to let them loose into a realm of pure thought that could never be related to anything concrete and actual. Instead of Christian meanings referring to an actually existing state of affairs, therefore, we were left with philosophical meanings referring to a purely speculative "reality." The result was that the philosophers created confusion by claiming that the abstract world brought into being by their speculative theories contained the *real* meaning of Christianity. On that account they did not hesitate to play fast and loose with the "what" of Christianity.

This process of subjecting Christianity to the yoke of Hegelian speculation was set forth at length by Kierkegaard in the *Concluding Unscientific Postscript*—showing that his viewpoint had not changed between 1837 and 1846, when the *Postscript* was published. In this book the pseudonymous Johannes Climacus, John the Climber, explained how philosophers now argue, in effect, "that it is not Christianity which is and was and remains the truth. . .no, it is the philosopher's understanding of Christianity that constitutes the truth of Christianity" (C.U.P., 200).

Using the example of the loss of belief in heaven, the *Postscript* (C.U.P., 323) said that "modern speculation" so understands Christianity that it has "about got back to paganism." The speculative movement "has strangely made the discovery that there is no 'beyond'" and that "notions of a future life, of another world, and similar ideas" are the products of "the dialectical limitations of the finite understanding." The result is that the conception of the future life has become something to joke about, causing us to look back with the complacency of superiority and smile at the time when this conception "transformed the whole of life."

Here one of the constituents of the "what" of Christianity, namely, belief in the "beyond," is assumed not to be in doubt for Christian thinking. It is not proved, of course, for it is *believed*. But the speculative thinker dismisses it as unbelievable. He has already decided that he has apprehended all the truth the concept of the future life contained, *and has gone further*. Since he knows himself to be finite and, though finite, yet capable of thinking about the infinite, he assumes that the "real" meaning of the beyond is the infinite in which he already participates in thought. Thus he puts behind him the notion of "another world" as a mistake arising from the finite understanding picturing the infinite inadequately by means of imagery drawn from finite existence; or, less politely, *sheer primitive mythology*.

For Kierkegaard, this is comic. The idealistic thinker imagines that reality necessarily conforms to the idea in his head; whereas the only kind of reality he encounters is actual existence, which does not conform to anything else, but is what it is. As a result, Kierkegaard says, one must take special precautions before entering into discussion with a philosophy of this sort:

> ...first to separate the philosopher from the philosophy, and then as in cases of black magic, witchcraft, and possession by the devil, to use a powerful formula of incantation to get the bewitched philosopher transformed into a particular existing human being, and thus restored back to his true state (C.U.P., 324).

It is because Christianity engages human beings in their true state that Kierkegaard argued all his days that you cannot go further and surpass it; though, of course, you are always free to bypass it and accept alternative readings of existence.

To bring the argument down to particulars, one constituent of the "what" of Christianity for Kierkegaard is revelation. God reveals to us in New Testament Christianity that which becomes the truth for us—for example, "the future life"—or else we should have no reason to believe it. In conformity with his feeling that he needed to take special precautions with speculative thinkers around, he avoided the word "revelation" in his writings (just as he avoided the word "supernatural" in speaking of the "beyond"). Instead, he spoke in the *Philosophical Fragments* of the situation of the existing individual being that of a learner who, if he "is to acquire the Truth, the Teacher must bring it to him; and not only so, but he must give him the condition necessary for understanding it" (P.F., 17). In explaining why this is the learner's situation, Kierkegaard was forced to use Biblical and theological language, explaining (with the aid of capitals and italics) how man, having his *Sin* made known to him by his *Judge,* nevertheless finds *Atonement* through a *Redeemer* who, bearing his *Guilt,* opens the way to *Conversion* through *Repentance,* and so to a *New Birth* (P.F., 19-23). Naming directly these Christian concepts was unavoidable at this place. *Philosophical Fragments* being "a project of thought" setting out to see whether the pagan consciousness—in the person of Socrates, its highest point—could be transcended, the evidence of where Christianity went further than paganism had to be displayed. The name of Christ was withheld, though, since the *Fragments* dealt with reflection, not edification.

Following the *Fragments,* and advancing to attempt a definition of Christianity, the *Postscript* also dealt with the concept of revelation while avoiding the word (precautions!). The problem being Christian truth, now that pagan consciousness was no longer the starting point, the central question was narrowed from how we are to relate ourselves to the truth to how we are to relate ourselves to God. John the Climber said that he was not a Christian, yet, unlike many who claimed that title, he knew what Christianity was. Therefore he knew that the Christian relationship to God came after a break with "immediacy." The Christian understands that God as Spirit, invisible and omnipresent, is never immediately available. God is found only in "inwardness." "The immediate relationship to God is paganism, and only after the breach had taken place can there be any question of a true God-relationship" (C.U.P., 218).

Speculative thinking was pagan. Why? Was it not also inward thinking, seeking the invisible God spiritually? The answer had been given already in Kierkegaard's letter of 1837, at the point where I discontinued the quotation (see page 46): There Kierkegaard explained how philosophers give Christian concepts "an entirely different general meaning."

...whereby faith becomes immediate certainty, which at bottom is neither more nor less than the vital fluid of the life of the mind, its atmosphere; tradition has become the summary of a certain world experience, whilst inspiration has become nothing but the result of God having breathed the spirit of life into man, and incarnation nothing else than the existence of one or other ideas in one or more individuals. ...(Dru, 89).

Speculative thinking represents a relapse into the pagan perspective because the existence of ideas in the philosopher's mind simply means that he can reflect, not that his reflections relate to any actual reality—his own individual existence, for example. If the philosopher imagines that God is present in his philosophical ideas, then he is trusting in an immediate relationship with God achieved through his capacity for reflection. He reflects and—immediately—God appears. The inwardness pertains wholly to the philosophy, in that it is a mental and not a sensory activity.

But separate the philosopher from the philosophy, and the conditions for true inwardness appear. We now ask, Is the philosopher—this existing individual—related to God through inwardness, or, as the Christian would say, through faith? The answer to that question is not available with immediate certainty or in such a way that it can be objectively demonstrated. God knows, since "before him no creature is hidden, but all are open and laid bare to the eyes of him with whom we have to do" (Heb. 4:13). We cannot know what is hidden in God, unless we learn it through our God-relationship. And, equally, we cannot probe the God-relationship of another. So this relationship involves us in true inwardness. It involves us in a "double reflection" where the object of reflection is nothing that we can know for ourselves, but that which God makes known to us, namely, how we in our existence stand in relationship to God. This knowledge is inward knowledge, and so subjective.

Thus reflection on existence means reflection on the subject of subjective thinking. And since there can be no truth that is anything more than proximate in relation to the truth of our existence vis-à-vis God, the subjective thinker is the only person who can approach the truth about Christianity. In the *Postscript* John the Climber lived up to his name by advancing upward to this final topic:

> That subjectivity, inwardness, is the truth; that existence is the decisive thing; that this was the path along which it was necessary to move in order to approach Christianity, which is precisely inwardness, though not any and every type of inwardness, whence it was necessary also to fix definitely and clearly the prior stages: this was my idea (C.U.P., 251).

An idea, of course, is not necessarily true. Christianity is not necessarily true because it is the truth for subjective thinking. The *Postscript* simply claimed that this is what Christianity is, true or not. And, given subjectivity as the principle of Christian truth, only living subjectively—in objective uncertainty, in "faith"—will resolve the issue.

> Without risk there is no faith. . . .If I wish to preserve myself in faith I must constantly be intent upon holding fast the objective uncertainty, so as to remain out upon the deep, over seventy thousand fathoms of water, still preserving my faith (C.U.P., 182).

It is now possible to see why Kierkegaard regarded the "what" of Christianity as being given in the "how." Christianity, demanding faith as its first condition, cannot just be a good idea to be commended because it gives a better explanation of the universe than rival ideas. It cannot even be properly expounded as the sum of the "truths" it presents for our belief. Certainly, "truths" are presented to the Christian (cf. the prologue to Luke's Gospel, where the purpose of the Gospel is said to be "that you may know the truth concerning the things of which you have been informed—Luke 1:4). But the "what" of Christianity, conceived as doctrinal statements defining orthodoxy, is an abstract paradigm unless it is seen in the light of the "how" demanding the commitment of the individual to its truth, as a living demand laid upon him in his concrete existence; unless, as Kierkegaard puts it, it drives the individual to subjectivity and inwardness. Its essential character is that it compels us to place passion and decision above the wish to know first and act afterwards—to place subjective above objective thinking, to view God himself always through his self-revelation to us in his *pro me*, as Luther said; or, as Kierkegaard said, as *infinite subjectivity*.

Here Kierkegaard's teaching is often represented as opening the door to an irrational and undirected emotionalism. Theodor Haecker, observing that Kierkegaard's dictum about the "what" of Christianity being given in the "how" was just "an afterthought," writes: "Enthusiasm is given absolute value, so that anyone evincing enthusiasm for a disgusting lie (as frequently happens) is 'truer' than one who clings soberly to 'truth' " *(Kierkegaard, the Cripple,* 17). Now, Kierkegaard does say: "The objective accent falls on WHAT is said, the subjective accent on HOW it is said" (C.U.P., 181); and he draws the conclusion that it is *religiously* truer to worship a false god with devotion than to pay lip service to the One True God. This is very different, however, from suggesting that truth is to be identified with strength of passion, or that all beliefs are self-justifying. Again, he does say:

> Here is a definition of truth: *An objective uncertainty held fast in an approximation-process of the most passionate inwardness is the truth,* the highest truth attainable for an *existing* individual" (C.U.P., 182).

But this definition hinges on the concept of "passionate inwardness"—which is hardly mere strong feelings, though strong feelings are essential to it. The quotation from the *Journals* I gave at the beginning of the chapter (page 42) indicates that Kierkegaard believed inwardness not to be at war with the objective (truth itself). His objection was to the misapplication of the "objective method" to subject matter to which it could not apply. Since subjective thinking sought the objective along its proper path, the complaints about Johannes Climacus being "purely subjective" were beside the point. Subjectivity in an existing individual had simply no connection with subjectivism as a general theory of knowledge or as a general philosophy of life.

Everything relates, here as elsewhere, to the use of dialectic. I pointed out in the last chapter that Socratic dialectic became Kierkegaard's chosen tool because he found it to be the way of thinking that does not fold itself in upon itself, but opens itself to the actual. Unlike the Hegelian dialectic, it imposes no closed pattern upon existence. Hegel's logic, by uniting thesis and antithesis in a synthesis which then becomes the thesis of a higher triad, creates a static pattern as the measure of all things. Hegel commanded the universe to jump through the hoops he held up before it—and was convinced the universe had obeyed. That is why Kierkegaard thought him a genius in speculation, and existentially comic. The dialectic Kierkegaard learnt from Socrates and other Greek thinkers (notably Aristotle), like other methods of reflection, attempts to tie the scattered elements of experience into a comprehensible unity. It is intellectually ambitious. Yet its saving grace is that it unites ambition with modesty and the realism that can smile at its failures. When it meets with actualities resisting the effort to bring them together, it leaves them disunited; and, though hoping to find a larger unity within which they will eventually be seen to agree, it refuses to announce the event beforehand.

Kierkegaard was no irrationalist. By any estimate he was a strenuous thinker; loving thought as part of life, yet never forgetting how thought exists to serve life, not vice versa. Faith for him was suprarational. He learned this chiefly from

Hamann and from Lessing, while adopting neither the romantic antirationalism of the former nor the detached stance ("without earnestness," said Kierkegaard) of the latter.[3] He accepted the need for faith as he accepted the conditions of historical existence, because faith was necessary for any individual taking his place in history. He wrote in the *Fragments*:

A contemporary may then safely use his eyes and so forth, but let him look to his conclusions. He cannot know, as a matter of immediate cognition, that his fact has come into existence, but neither can he know it as a matter of necessity; for the very first expression for coming into existence is a breach of continuity (P.F., 104).

What Kierkegaard asserts here is the difference between logical and historical knowledge. All that comes into existence is in the process of becoming, and so lacks the certainty belonging to ideas which are the same always for every one. When an individual asserts anything at all about the historical world, he appeals to what he himself sees and believes. Yet any "fact" in the realm of history may be disputed. Thus the individual asserts what is, indeed, "his" fact; and others are free to reject it. Whether he will persist in continuing to believe as he does about "his" fact, when others doubt it, will depend not upon his knowledge but upon his *passion*—how much it means to him and how strongly he is convinced of the truth of what he asserts. The skeptic, says Kierkegaard, illustrates this procedure. He, no more than any other man, has knowledge of the true meaning of human existence. He keeps himself secure in his skeptical conclusions about the way things happen simply by an act of his own will. He will not be convinced otherwise, because he does not wish to be. Argument about the facts is futile so long as the man remains unchanged.

It follows that faith in anything historical (from one's own existence to the truth of Christianity) means commitment—"not so much a conclusion as a resolution," said Kierkegaard—and on that account a belief excluding doubt. Doubt is always present, though present as rejected where belief is.

. . .when faith resolves to believe it runs the risk of committing itself to an error, but it nevertheless believes. There is no other road to faith; if one wishes to escape risk, it is as if one wanted to know with certainty that he can swim without going into the water (P.F., 103 footnote).

Dialectical thinking meant for Kierkegaard accepting the complete duality of knowledge and belief, united only by their being two activities of the same person capable of living, using his senses, reflecting. In the *Postscript* he developed the opposition between knowing immediately ("objectively") and believing. "If I am capable of grasping God objectively, I do not believe, but precisely because I cannot do this I must believe" (C.U.P., 182). A believed truth, by the same token, is paradoxical, unacceptable to the mind which insists upon knowing objectively; and therefore it approaches the "absurd." Beliefs need not seem absurd, of course, but neither can they be altogether reasonable, or they would be universally accepted by reasonable men; so they remain to some degree paradoxical. An example here might be the existence of individuals. Nearly everyone agrees that belief in the "real" existence of you and me and other people is a sane kind of belief, although solipsism is a logical possibility; and the belief that individuality is no more than a surface phenomenon, and that ultimately all consciousness is "really" one, has always had a respectable following, because every rational defense of individuality runs into deep difficulties.

Granted that it often seems to be "reasonable" to accept a few loopholes in reason by the way, yet the fact remains that the reflecting mind cannot conceive of reality being essentially incoherent, or of truth being self-contradictory. Kierkegaard did not deny this. He wrote in the *Postscript:* "But the eternal essential truth is by no means a paradox; but it becomes paradoxical by virtue of its relationship to an existing individual" (C.U.P., 183). What he insisted upon was that the paradoxical nature of existential truths must be faced squarely and admitted to be essential to our reflection upon the actual conditions of our life. And then he went on to say something still more. He said that Christianity demanded faith that was prepared to admit not just the paradoxical but the absurd—the Absolute Paradox. The Christian belief in a historical event called the Incarnation involved making statements that caused thought to reel. The confession of the Christian that God had become man, the Eternal come into time, drove home in the sharpest possible way that Christianity is an intellect offense and actually repellent to the reason. Already in the letter of 1837 Kierkegaard had rejected the current philosophical notion that the concept of incarnation had to do with the (divine) idea coming into men (see page 50). He expanded the same opinion in *Training in Christianity,* the work of 1850 "authored" by Anti-Climacus (the pseudonym indicating one who was the opposite of John the Climber, one who *was* a Christian and spoke out of faith). In this book he connected the "offence" with the Pharisees' being offended with the teaching of Jesus (Matt. 15:12), and also with the words of Jesus, "Blessed is he, whosoever shall not be offended in me" (Matt. 11:6). He wrote:

> The God-Man is not the unity of God and mankind. Such terminology exhibits the profundity of optical illusion. The God-Man is the unity of God and an individual man. That the human race is or should be akin to God is ancient paganism; but that an individual man is God is Christianity, and this individual man is the God-Man. There is neither in heaven, nor on earth, nor in the depths, nor in the aberrations of the most fantastic thinking, the possibility of a (humanly speaking) more insane combination (T.I.C., 84).

For Kierkegaard the Absolute Paradox of the God-Man was, of course, more than a "Christian concept," more than something belonging to the "what" of Christianity. It was that. But it was also, in its challenge to the reason by virtue of being the absurd, a discovery of subjectivity, a relationship to the God-Man made possible through double reflection communicating the gift of faith. Thus, through subjective thinking, it belonged to the "how" of Christianity. To accept the Absolute Paradox demanded "the utmost passionate inwardness" and the most resolute turning towards existence and away from the "objectivity" of speculation.

It is highly relevant to remember how Kierkegaard was attracted to Socrates because he kept close to existence in his teaching. He did not remain a "he," hiding from living the consequences of his thinking, but became an "I" (see page 35). There is another reference in the *Journals* to the difference between the third and the first person.

> The opposite of antiquity, which used the third person of itself, because one's life was merely a fact, is to risk everything by saying 'I', to say the highest thing about oneself directly. That is expressed in the God-Man; he would not be the God-Man if he were great in such a way as to become third person (Dru, 975).

The God-Man is the one to whom the Christian believer is related through faith, precisely because he is first person and makes the believer encounter him as first person also.

Kierkegaard elaborated this thought in the concept of being "contemporaneous" with Christ. The first disciples, he said, had no advantage over those who were to follow, because although they were in the presence of the God-Man, faith in him was no easier for them than it is for us. They knew him as someone sharing their external environment, yet, perhaps for that very reason, did not encounter him in a first-person relationship.

The concept of "contemporaneousness" appeared in the *Fragments* and in *Training in Christianity* became a leading theme. The book opens on this note.

> It is eighteen hundred years and more since Jesus Christ walked here on earth. . . .But so long as there is a believer, such a one must, in order to become such, have been, and as a believer must continue to be, just as contemporary with His presence on earth as were those first contemporaries. This contemporaneousness is the condition of faith, and more closely defined it is faith (T.I.C., 9).

Such a statement gives us the light in which we should read the definition of Christianity given in the *Postscript*, where Kierkegaard wrote:

Christianity is not a doctrine but an existential communication expressing an existential contradiction. . . .To assume that this denial that Christianity is a doctrine should imply that Christianity is contentless, is merely a *chicane*. When the believer exists in his faith his existence acquires tremendous content, but not in the sense of paragraph-material (C.U.P., 339-40).

For the believer to exist "in his faith" means his becoming contemporaneous with Christ, becoming an "I" and living the paradox of faith, discovering that Christianity is at once suffering and joy. Reflection upon existence can tell us what Christianity is. It will not turn a Johannes Climacus into an Anti-Climacus, for that required an actual venturing far out over the seventy thousand fathoms of water. The difference between understanding the meaning of faith and having faith is a whole existence of difference.

Interlude:
Pause for Looking Around

IT MAY BE CONVENIENT at this point to look back along the road traveled so far, and to pause a moment before going on again.

In the *Postscript* Johannes Climacus put forward and defended two theses: (A) a logical system is possible; (B) an existential system is impossible (C.U.P., 99-113). As Kierkegaard addressed himself to the task of becoming an existential thinker, there is no system to be discovered in his writings. He himself indicated their nature when talking about existential thought:

> When it is impossible to think existence, and the existing individual nevertheless thinks, what does this signify? It signifies that he thinks intermittently, that he thinks before and after. His thought cannot attain to absolute continuity. It is only in a fantastic sense that an existing individual can be constantly *sub specie aeterni*[1] (C.U.P., 293).

There is plenty of coherence in Kierkegaard's authorship—as I hope I have been able to convey—but not that striving after "absolute continuity" marking out the true system-builder. Thinking before and after, he turned his attention to those aspects of existence which had been of particular importance to him, and upon which he believed all men, and his own generation especially, needed to reflect earnestly.

The would-be commentator on Kierkegaard thus has the task of picking up a sufficient number of the themes developed in various places throughout the authorship and bringing these together for comment. From this labor a reader will gain some idea of the meaning of the author's leading concepts and be equipped to turn to the works themselves without being halted constantly by unfamiliar terms.

In that area of duty I have been most remiss. There has been no mention in all this time of such vital Kierkegaardian specialties as "Anxiety" (*Angst*), "the Leap," "the Moment," "Possibility," "Repetition," "Transition," and so on; and even the "Spheres of Existence" ("Stages")—of such importance in the whole authorship that they are frequently introduced first—have not been called out of the wings to make their bow under the spotlight.

My excuse for this seeming negligence is that I think Kierkegaard's words about the "what" of Christianity being given in the "how" apply, by analogy, to his authorship also. His subject, after all, was Christianity. If we know how he approached Christian faith, and how he judged Hegelianism to have misread that faith, his coinage of special terms will present little difficulty. He was concerned, as he said, "to obtain a little peace for the weary Christian terminology. . . unfathomable and calmly profound as it is in itself, but made breathless and almost unmeaning in current usage" (C.U.P., 324). Furthermore, this terminology, he added, had been taken over by speculative thought and made captive to its own purposes. He was willing to take a lesson from the enemy in this war; and, in fact, made a good many raids into Hegelian territory in particular, bringing back word-prisoners to work for him in an "existential" environment in place of a "speculative" one. But he did not mind where he discovered suitable new words to stand in for exhausted ones, provided that they could serve the turn where needed.

So the real question is always how Kierkegaard used his concepts rather than what they looked like, for without an understanding of the "how" the "what" would almost inevitably be misinterpreted. I shall have more to say of this in the chapters still to come, where the way Kierkegaard's writings have been used is investigated. Just now, though, it may be worth while looking briefly at the Kierkegaardian Spheres of Existence and at his definition of existence in order to see how, as always, he brings his terms into the service of a Christian perspective.

In his *Phenomenology of Mind* Hegel elaborated three "stages" of mankind's consciousness: (A) consciousness at the level of sense experience; (B) self-consciousness rising to the appreciation of law and reason; (C) reason, "a stage of mind" aiming to "become completely conscious of its own nature." Kierkegaard proposed his own three stages: (A) the aesthetic (dominated by self-gratification); (B) the ethical (obedient to the absolute as law); (C) the religious (obedient to the absolute as grace). While Hegel thought the stages of consciousness to be strictly successive and working out in the process of world history, Kierkegaard insisted that there was no "necessity" compelling anyone to go through the three in turn. Everything depended on choice.

Either/Or, the first book of the authorship, began with the aesthetic view of life. Its first sentence asked: "What is a poet?"—and it carried prefixed to its two volumes mottos from Edward Young and Chateaubriand, writers popular among the romantics, who stood for the aesthetic attitude par excellence. Yet the reason for starting here was not that this is where most of us begin life, though that may be true enough, too. Kierkegaard's own explanation was ". . .Christianity is very far behind. One must begin with paganism. And so I begin with *Either/Or*" (Dru, 734). Later, in order to emphasize that the Stages were not stages in evolutionary development, he renamed them "Spheres" when referring to them in the *Postscript.*

Either/Or posed the question in relation to love: *either* aesthetic drifting in the erotic as an end in itself, *or* the moral choice of marriage in which the erotic was transcended in family love. But the choice did not end there; for the final section of *Either/Or* was headed "Ultimatum," and took the form of a sermon leading to the declaration that there is no stopping on the road to true happiness short of facing the question of salvation. Two years later, *Stages on Life's Way* took the same argument further, ending on the note that, as life forced the individual to face suffering, so the only resolution of human suffering was the forgiveness of human sin.

The Stages or Spheres of Existence illustrate Kierkegaard's conviction that religion is no casual option for those who happen to have a taste for it, or who need some compensation for limitations laid on them—an opiate for pain—or who turn to it in their old age when they have exhausted the pleasures of life. Life presents everyone with an either-or on which his happiness depends absolutely. Beyond the aesthetic snatching at pleasures as they go by, which is refusal to choose, lies the possibility of living for an infinite value. That means ceasing to live simply as a member of the human species and finding oneself as an individual capable of directing his life to an infinite value. The great divide, therefore, lies between the either-or of the aesthetic and the ethical religious. Yet, once that divide has been crossed, further choices lie ahead. The ethical sphere opens into the religious, which reveals itself to be another either-or. Individuals must choose again, taking the way either of a natural type of God-consciousness which Kierkegaard calls "Religion A," or of "Religion B," Christian revelation involving the Absolute Paradox.

If we reject each higher choice offered to us along life's way, we destroy ourselves.

This brings into the picture Kierkegaard's definition of existence. In the *Postscript* he offered this definition: "Existence is a synthesis of the infinite and the finite, and the existing individual is both infinite and finite" (C.U.P., 350). This definition explains why the aesthetic life cannot offer the individual happiness. To cling to it is to deny the infinite, which will not allow us to rest in the finite, and so is to tear ourselves apart in self-contradiction.

Once again, we see how Kierkegaard adopted the terminology of idealistic philosophy, while transforming its meaning. For Hegel mankind was the finite expression of Infinite

Spirit. Existence represents the alienation of the finite from the infinite, a "self-othering" of the divine in which man, through consciousness of his alienation, must grow into that full self-consciousness of the identity of God and man which brings him to make himself into what he is. In apparent agreement with Hegel, Kierkegaard wrote, in *Sickness Unto Death,* "Man is spirit." But then he immediately added: "But what is spirit? Spirit is the self. . . .So regarded, man is not yet a self" (S.U.D., 146).

The speculative misunderstanding of Christianity, so Kierkegaard never tired of insisting, lay in its assumption that contradictions could be reconciled through the power of the idea. Existence lost its brokenness through being viewed *sub specie aeterni,* and appeared as a perfectly logical and understandable process when interpreted as world history, whence it emerged as the life history of the Absolute. In such a perspective Christianity was a true, but imperfectly expressed, communication of the truths which speculation was able to grasp directly in their entirety. When man knew that he was finite spirit, then what Christianity taught about the Incarnation having resulted in the gift of the Holy Spirit became plain: the illusory distinction between the human and the divine was annulled. Yet, if man is not yet a self, and on that account not yet spirit, existence cannot be so easily "explained" and taken up into the speculative rationality of world history; the individual cannot be merged into general humanity; and the Christian message of sin and salvation cannot be "objectively" translated into terms avoiding the "subjective" dimension of passionate choice involving eternal consequences. The Holy Spirit, who for Christianity is the gift of the Incarnate God-Man, is not to be understood as the immanent self-consciousness of enlightened humanity.

In Kierkegaard's view, speculative thought, by bypassing concrete existence with its involvement in subjectivity, proved itself to have chosen to remain in the aesthetic stage. The philosopher who had confused himself with his philosophy, and who had relegated existence to a short paragraph within his System, remained a prisoner within the web of abstract thinking he had spun around himself to protect himself from actuality, its agonizing decisions and its unavoidable sufferings. His situation, intellectually considered, was comic. Existentially it was tragic. The eternal happiness which Christianity promised for the individual who dared to become himself, through accepting the Absolute Paradox of faith in passionate inwardness, had been rejected in favor of a purely imaginary certainty based on fantasy alone. The "what" of Christianity has been lost by a failure to understand that the "what" is given in the "how." For knowledge of the truth cannot be mediated through our claim to see as God sees, *sub specie aeterni,* but as God has willed it to be known in the truth that came through the historical mediation of one existing individual, Jesus Christ.

The gulf separating the aesthetic and the Christian interpretation of life is not only something essential for understanding Kierkegaard's teaching. It is also of the highest importance for estimating the legacy of his teaching for our day.

IV
The Age of the Crowd

THERE IS AN IMPRESSION AROUND that Kierkegaard, shut up alone with his broodings upon the individual and the otherworldliness of Christianity, had nothing to say about the social and cultural dimensions of life. This picture is a thoroughly distorted one.

The fact that Kierkegaard's authorship was designed to meet the cultural situation created by the Enlightenment, and its development in romanticism and idealism, is enough to prove that his thought was hardly cultivated in a vacuum. *The Point of View* lets us see how closely he viewed his work in relation to the events of his time. He always said that he spoke for Christianity "without authority," being neither priest, nor prophet, nor apostle. But he insisted that he had a task which he alone could carry out, and he described his work as a "corrective." He was to open his contemporaries' minds to truths which they had ignored because of their cultural situation and consequent immersion in the currents of the times.

Politically, the age was exciting. During Kierkegaard's lifetime the ideas set in motion by the French and American Revolutions were on the march and resulting in the end of absolute monarchies across the face of Europe. The theories of socialism and communism were the products of this period. The year 1848 (the year of the Communist Manifesto) was the year of revolutions, bringing upheavals and changes in Denmark also—war with Germany and an internal bloodless revolution. Kierkegaard believed his task to be to discover the roots of the happenings going on around him, being convinced, as he wrote in his essay "A Word about the

Relation of My Literary Activity to 'The Individual' " (using large letters for emphasis), "that this was an age of dissolution" (P.O.V., 132).

Conservative himself by temperament and training, Kierkegaard felt that in the welcome given to the idea of revolution—"the year '48, it stood for progress"—there was audible "the shrill rasping note which announces chaos." While claiming that he stood neither beside "the established order" nor against it, he also argued that "even the most mediocre 'establishment' is preferable to and higher than the vaguest of all vague conceptions, 'the multitude' " (O.A.R., 193). Yet his conservative reaction was no unfeeling denial of the need for political reform, and he specifically spelled out that his concept of "the multitude" was not one opposing the aristocracy to the plebs. The dissolution he saw and gave warning of was of a much more fundamental nature. The Christian qua Christian, he believed, had no right to lay down the law on political organization or to fight for political ends. But, equally, he was deeply involved in the current self-understanding of man that produced the spirit of the age with its inevitable political consequences.

In the letter of 1837 which I quoted in the previous chapter, Kierkegaard began by saying that, while Europe stood in fear of coming bankruptcy, a more far-reaching bankruptcy was threatening the age: "a confusion in language itself, a rebellion, and the most dangerous of all, the rebellion of words themselves, which torn from the dominion of man, rush upon one another in despair." Next, he went on to characterize the *idée fixe* of the whole age" as the determination to get "beyond"[1] the man ahead. With this he linked the rise and fall of fashions in philosophy and in literature, the whole being geared not to the need for being understood but to "the speed of the printing press" (Dru, 88).

We today, who hear so much about the breakdown in communication, can understand Kierkegaard's concern—and also wonder at the insight bringing him to put this item of the bankruptcy of words first on the list. Out of his belief that meaning must not be allowed to be squeezed out of words by the meretricious use of language came his struggle to find the proper form of communicating his authorship. Out of that struggle his dialectic was born. But, when looking for the cause of this recent loss of the integrity of language, he put it down to the ruling spirit of the generation that must prove its superiority before an audience, that must go "beyond," and therefore was in a rush to move without knowing where it was going. It all amounted to one thing, namely, *the triumph of quantitative thinking over qualitative*. The difference between these two types he tried to nail down with his contrasting concepts of "the single individual" and "the crowd" ("the multitude," "the masses," "the public").

The concept of the individual had its beginning in the Preface to the *Two Edifying Discourses,* the "religious" work accompanying the "aesthetic" work, *Either/Or.* There he referred to "that individual whom with joy and gratitude I call *my* reader," and "toward whom it [the book]," as it were, "stretches out its arms" (E.D., I, 5). Since Kierkegaard hoped that his books would be read by Regine, and understood by her to be saying what he could not tell her face to face, it may well have been this personal intention that gave the first impetus to his use of the concept to indicate the human person in his unique personhood—the "I"—as opposed to the human unit discovered by counting heads or asking for signatures.[2]

Nothing could be more wrongheaded than to assume that Kierkegaard's concept of single individual indicates an atomistic view of humanity. Certainly, he wished to have "the masses" broken down so that the individual could stand forth. But, equally, he knew that the separate human being cannot be an individual just by standing apart. He must be willing to undergo the discipline of *becoming* an individual. Thus, far from making community impossible, the individual is the sole basis upon which community can be built. The concept of individual*ism* is something else again. Fundamentally it is the product of Romanticism, embodying the exaltation of the self-will that glories in being utterly unique and bound to no laws except those this willful being decides shall hold for him—the apotheosis of the aesthetic refusal to become a responsible "I." Because of his lonely position, partly the result of his "melancholy" and partly of his need to follow his exceptional vocation (the "exceptional" is another of his concepts!), Kierkegaard never worked out the conditions of true community. But, especially in the *Works of Love,* he pointed to the foundation of Christian ethics in the duty of neighbor-love within the imperfect structures of human society.

He spoke of the concept of the individual and the concept of the either/or as the really important discoveries of his thought. It is not surprising to find that he believed he found in Socrates (who was called "the oddest one") the only previous use of "the individual," and in Hegel its antithesis. He wrote in the *Journals:*

> How often have I shown that fundamentally Hegel makes men into heathens, *into a race of animals gifted with reason.* For in the animal world 'the individual' is always less important than the race. But it is the peculiarity of the human race that just because the individual is created in the image of God 'the individual' is above the race.
>
> This can be wrongly understood and terribly misused: *concedo.* But that is Christianity. And *that* is where the battle must be fought (Dru, 1050).

Linking the concept of the individual with that of subjectivity, Kierkegaard pointed out that Hegel's philosophy, which wished to put religious truth under the control of "objective" reason, also abolished man's essential humanity. A race of animals gifted with reason was what the age had come to accept as being final, objective truth. The result was that the human search for quality within existence—and, with it, human growth in understanding through experiencing joyfulness and suffering (existential pathos)—was being explained away and replaced by subhuman categories of a quantitative type. The individual was submerged within "the generation"—a collective that found its identity (such as it was) in the fact that it had got "beyond" the previous generation and so, by quantitative reasoning, must be superior to it.

In his earlier years Kierkegaard spoke with great respect of the natural sciences. While recognizing that his own interests lay in another direction, in exploring the realms of reason and freedom, he saw how the study of science could lead to serene delight in the pursuit of truth that was wholly admirable. But later he gave the warning that the wholesale adoption of scientific attitude to life was destroying human values by bringing a quantifying approach to everything. The fault lay, he said, in the attempt to popularize the scientific spirit. In 1850 he wrote: "It is clear enough that 'this generation' tends to put natural science in the place of religion" (Dru, 1036). The ambitions of men in a generation where everyone was scrambling to get "beyond" everyone else had exploited science for an alien purpose.

What Kierkegaard knew in the green wood, we have come to know in the dry. The whole development of a global mass society built on a technology fed by scientific research has come about since his lifetime. The end result of the process he described could not have been imagined precisely in the mid-nineteenth century, because of the magnitude of the changes that have taken place. Yet, were Kierkegaard to be transported into our own day, it would be the rate of change alone, and not its direction, that would surprise him. He was, after all, the man who commented on the "fantastic" quality of the idealistic way of looking at the world. And so he would be prepared for fantastic developments in a culture dedicated to progress at an ever-quickening pace—quantitatively. That we are presently getting ready to send men to populate other planets—always provided that we escape destroying our own planet first; that millions are starving although we have the resources to bring plenty within the reach of all; that we preach equality, yet go in fear that the rapidly increasing disparity between the rich and the poor will lead to wars within nations and between continents: none of this would seem inconceivable to Kierkegaard.

Had he not already detected, in a small ripple of violence which hardly upset the middle-class life of Copenhagen, the shrill rasping note announcing chaos?

In *The Present Age,* part of a long article *A Literary Review* published in 1846, Kierkegaard wrote that the dialectic of antiquity had tended toward leadership (the great individual and the masses—the free man and the slave), while the dialectic of Christendom tended towards representation (the majority seeing its self-consciousness reflected in a representative). The dialectic of the present age, he added, tended toward equality, which led logically though mistakenly to a leveling "as the negative unity of the negative reciprocity of all individuals" (P.A., 52). And then he went on to comment: "The levelling process is not the action of an individual but the work of reflection in the hands of an abstract power" (P.A., 54).

It is here that Kierkegaard helps us to put into perspective so much of what has been happening since his "present age" and ours. What he called "reflection in the hands of an abstract power" we have come to know as ideology, and no insignificant part of our contemporary problems has arisen from the fact that the world is divided into ideological camps, between which there seems no possibility of reconciliation; because the clash is not between human beings who can respect one another as such, but between rival varieties of "abstract power" that can never meet.

It was Karl Marx who coined the term "ideology" in its present usage, and Marxism sprang out of Hegelianism. The interesting fact is that, when Marx decided that the task of philosophy must be to change the world and not merely to describe it, he carried with him the Hegelian assumption that philosophy describes "reality." The result was to set loose in the world the conviction that one ideology is the totally true one and that all the others are totally false, to be suppressed by liquidating those who support them. In Kierkegaardian terms, Marx united the passions of the ethical and the aesthetic stages of life. The aesthetic pathos, Kierkegaard said, is in words (the poet describes, he need not believe what he says), while the ethical pathos is in deeds. Moreover, since the ethical stage already stands within view of the religious, the party that is sure that it has the right to act decisively on behalf of the truth cannot hold back from claiming that it has the Absolute (God or a God-substitute) on its side. In 1849 Kierkegaard, in an uncannily perceptive note in his *Papers,* put down his conviction that, as at the time of the Reformation what appeared to be religious movements turned out afterwards to be political movements, so "now everything appears to be politics but will explicate itself as a religious movement."[3] Religion, once more, is seen not to be a doctrine but a passionate commitment. The denial of God does not mean an absence of religious pathos (which is a transformation of the self expressing its commitment). Only, since this religion is not experienced as inwardness, it issues in consigning others to destruction instead of finding salvation for oneself.

The crowd, Kierkegaard insisted, *is untruth.* He said so because the crowd represents the loss of the individual, the human, and the embracing of abstractions instead of actual existence. While he thought of abstractions principally in the form of pure speculation, rather than in the form of *applied* speculation we know as ideology, he also knew that it could regress back beyond thought to thoughtlessness. Hegel had taught men to believe themselves to be animals with reason. They might then behave on occasion simply as animals, the human element submerged entirely in herd feeling. There is an entry in the *Journals* for 1850 where Kierkegaard said he would like to write a book: *On diabolic possession in modern times.* This would

> show how mankind *en masse* gives itself up to evil, how nowadays it happens *en masse.* That is why people flock together, in order that natural and animal hysteria should get hold of them, in order to feel themselves stimulated, enflamed and *ausser sich* . . . where the pleasure consists in losing oneself in order to be volatised into a higher potency, where being outside oneself hardly knows what one is

doing or saying, or who or what is speaking through one, while the blood courses faster, the eyes are bright and staring, the passions and lust seething.

O depths of confusion and depravity, when it is at the same time values as the seriousness of life, warm-heartedness, love, yes even— Christianity (Dru, 1063).

Thus the passions excluded by Hegelian speculation return in perverted form. Vitalism replaces rationalism. Yet it is abstraction still. The Hitler rallies were moved by the Leader's oratory because, for the crowds gathered there, he was not an individual but the symbol of the German Spirit, the incarnation of the *Volk*. And mass hysteria means the loss of the individual. Thus William Faulkner accurately describes a lynching party as "not faces but a face, not a mass nor even a mosaic of them but a Face."

The Present Age described the time as one preferring reflection to action and incapable of acting with passion. On this account Kierkegaard has often been accused of ignoring the fact that his age was one of real revolutionary enthusiasm and the moment when a new era of hope for the downtrodden masses was emerging. That may be so. Yet on the other hand he pointed to a very real characteristic of the modern era, and one which permeates our contemporary existence, when he wrote that enthusiasm is the unifying principle of a revolutionary age, and envy the negative unifying principle of a reflective and passionless one. A reflective age may well break out into violent revolt; but afterwards it will relapse into apathy again. Rebellion, he said, is like the eruption of a volcano drowning every other sound. The leveling process is "a deathly silence in which one can hear one's heart beat, a silence which nothing can pierce, in which everything is engulfed, powerless to resist . . . the leveling process in modern times, corresponds, in reflection, to fate in antiquity" (P.A., 51-52).

It would be hard to better this description of the hopelessness that alternates in contemporary society with the fevered expectation that Utopia may be just round the corner, if only we can get "beyond" today fast enough. The deathly silence is

[72]

given many names. It is referred to as boredom, alienation, the death wish, wanting to get out of the rat race, hopelessness, meaninglessness, psychic trauma, depersonalization. Kierkegaard traced it to one source: the victory of abstraction over the individual. And he said that, since it was inspired by envy, it had one outcome: brutality.

The brutality he had in mind was mild enough to make us smile. He expected he might have his hat knocked off his head! Yet, since he called the process "diabolical" and given over to the power of evil, it could obviously end with the slaughter, in conditions of fiendish cruelty, of eight million Jews—explained dispassionately in true abstract fashion as "the solution to the Jewish problem." In Kierkegaard's eyes, the result of the lack of passion belonging to the leveling process was that no one was responsible—since no one was ever present except in the third person, as an onlooker who always had the excuse that whatever happened happened when he wasn't looking. Kierkegaard's judgment has been only too well confirmed by the Eichmann trial. There it was impossible to overlook the horror of the fact that the enormity of the crimes being described seemed to have no relation to the man in the dock, a completely unremarkable figure looking like any anonymous official, sitting in detachment and making notes as though for a committee report.

Brutality is what civilization exists to eradicate. Christendom was able to claim considerable advance in the elimination of the barbarous and the introduction of urbane ("city-like") manners. The Enlightenment looked back with a shudder at the Christian Dark Ages when, as Hegel said, the priest and the despot had conspired to hold men in ignorance. Today, after two World Wars, and surrounded by hot and cold conflicts and the clamor of groups shouting (not politely) for power, we still hope for the advancement of freedom and urbanity in society. But we have learnt since the Enlightenment that civilization does not tread a straight path upward from ignorance into full consciousness of the knowledge of good and evil, bringing us inevitably to realize our true humanity. We have found that the city can breed brutality as well as culture, that technological

[73]

progress frustrates as well as advances personal freedom, that men will sell themselves and betray their nation for a political idea held as an absolute ("religious") truth, and that despotic rule can be chosen by an educated as well as by an ignorant people.

However strongly recent experience may demonstrate the opposite, we are still apt to think that brutality today must be a hangover from earlier semicivilized times. Evolutionary thinking here, nevertheless, is unprofitable. Kierkegaard, a determined enemy of the theory of cultural evolution (world-historical thinking), was more realistic in tying brutality to the negative passion of envy. The brutal person is one who wishes enviously to hurt another, perhaps in the most sophisticated way of crucifying him on the cross of polite condescension, if it is not politic to crucify him actually. Thus brutality belongs properly not to an unreflective state but is a spiritual condition, generated by hatred of excellence in another that, by existing, compels people to feel its nonexistence in themselves.

Kierkegaard related the prevalence of envy to the standard of values introduced by the leveling process. Such a process ignored the ethical—the recognition of infinite responsibility in the individual—because, having abolished the individual, it introduced the customs of the "crowd" instead. Today we have become familiar with a somewhat similar set of ideas through David Riesman, author of *The Lonely Crowd.* Dr. Riesman uses the sociological categories of "outer-directed" and "inner-directed" personalities. Kierkegaard, however, takes his stand wholly on the ethical.

Hegel's System was remarkable, said Kierkegaard, because it did not require any section on ethics; and he saw the disappearance of ethics all along the line. In 1846 he wrote in his *Journals:* "In the end physics will displace ethics just as metaphysics displaced theology. The modern statistical view of ethics contributes toward that" (Dru, 562). If the consciousness of mankind is evolving toward an objective understanding of reality, then it follows logically that ethical ideas are relative to some particular stage of social development, and the wish to assert any ethical norm after it has fallen into disuse (statistics!) must be an antiprogressive "subjective" error. Totalitarian systems automatically subsume ethical standards under the dogmatic pronouncements of party ideology, dismissing private ethical judgments as "sentiment." Kierkegaard's experience, and so his concern, was with the "free" society that we know as ours, where public opinion takes the place of the party line, yet is based on remarkably similar assumptions. Kierkegaard compared the ethical consciousness of his day to the child sent off to a party and told to conduct himself by doing just what he sees the other children do.

A widely accepted norm of behavior at the present time is that you should do what you feel like doing "so long as it doesn't hurt anyone else." Yet, if envy is, as Kierkegaard believed, the hidden quality underlying our age of "the third person," then even this reduction of ethical norms to aesthetic preferences is suspect from the beginning. It assumes a capacity for objectivity which has all the marks of the comic which Kierkegaard believed to inhere in all claims to possess the objective "idea."

It is interesting, also, to see how thinking today about norms of conduct tends to split into opposing paths: on the one hand we find the romantic claim that the aesthetics must be totally free from social control; for instance, that hallucinating drugs must be freely available for those who wish to explore a "personal" vision. And on the other hand we find an approximation to the Hegelian belief that Freedom is achieved through the Spirit in man overcoming all material obstacles to the realization of the Idea, so that right is established through the achievement of power in society. We are becoming familiar with groups who demand recognition for their group cause by demonstrating that they are prepared to use power (brutally if need be) to gain their end. While this may be the result of the failure of our mass society to allow sections of the community to find a tolerable way of life within it, the phenomenon recalls Kierkegaard's caustic remark: "Simply in order to put a passing whim into practice a few people add themselves together, and the thing is done—then they dare to do it" (P.A., 53). Perhaps Kierkegaard played down the fact that sometimes things have to be done, even by irregular means, by people who care enough to do it. But his continual concern—and it is surely no trivial one—was that the responsibility which each individual must bear for himself should not be shuffled off by the expedient of hiding in the crowd, that essentially irresponsible monster.

In *The Present Age* Kierkegaard said he would permit himself to be called a prophet, though only "in the modern sense" of prognosticator (P.A., 85-86). Since he certainly foresaw with considerable clarity many of the disillusionments we were later to experience, and some of the issues we still find hard to disentangle, we would be ungenerous to withhold the title from him. Pre-eminently, though, he was a communicator. And it is in the area of communication that he has something particularly valuable, I believe, to say to us.

"A revolutionary age," he wrote, "is an age of action; ours is the age of advertisement and publicity" (P.A., 35). He said that without having a single roadside billboard, illuminated sign, T.V. commercial, or publicity agent. He built his case on the argument that the "generation" has supplanted the individual as the director of society, that the "generation" is represented in an abstraction called "the public," and that the public is created by another abstraction called "the press." The conclusion of his argument is that a nation's policy, tastes, morals, and opinions on everything from the existence of God to the number of buttons a person should have on his coat is decided—how or by whom nobody quite knows. But the popular explanation given, and believed, is that public opinion has been made known through the press.

Now Kierkegaard was altogether prejudiced about the press through his experience with the lively though not altogether irresponsible satirical paper *The Corsair*. The editor

Goldschmidt, through a personal regard for him, had not included him among the celebrities picked out for special treatment until Kierkegaard himself forced his hand. Then a series of cruel caricatures in *The Corsair* made Kierkegaard an object of derision in the streets.

Yet, as so often when his prejudices were aroused, he saw the press with brilliant clarity. Finding that "public opinion" was not formed by solid facts or rational judgment, he concluded that the press existed to stimulate the *negative* passions (envy in leading place) that prevented people from becoming individuals. Without inwardness and passion, men's minds were occupied with *talkativeness, gossip, formlessness, superficiality, flirtation,* and *reasoning* (as opposed to dialectic). The point of this list, which Kierkegaard gave in *The Present Age,* is that every item on it indicates a confusion of opposites (like Hegel's principle of mediation). Thus talkativeness forgets the virtues of both words and silence, and consequently makes words meaningless and prevents the cultivation of silence from which alone inwardness can be gained. But, though qualitatively disastrous, quantitatively talkativeness rates very highly: it fills time.

Marshall McLuhan's slogan, "the medium is the message," is universally quoted these days. The essential insight contained in that slogan was familiar to Kierkegaard. In the *Postscript* he wrote:

> The mode of apprehension of the truth is precisely the truth. It is therefore untrue to answer a question in a medium in which the question cannot arise (C.U.P., 287).

The difference between McLuhan's view of communication and Kierkegaard's, though, is that Kierkegaard was not mesmerized as we are by the quantitative and "objective" aspects of our culture. When McLuhan talks about media he thinks first of all of technical presentation, e.g., the printed page as against the recorded voice or picture, and then of the social effect, e.g., the printed page develops the solitary reader thinking in "linear" terms, but T.V. brings us back into the tribe, allowing us to feel rather than to think, and to experience "involvement in depth." Kierkegaard never assumed that a medium of communication is defined adequately in external terms alone, since meaning is not something external. Words on a page, for instance, do not constitute a single medium. They can be used to convey meanings on a whole range of different dimensions. The words *you are doomed to die* convey utterly different messages in a letter from a homicidal maniac, a letter from a friend with medical knowledge, a short story, and a devotional treatise.

The anxiety Kierkegaard felt at the beginning of his career over the loss of the meaning of words was anxiety over the possible loss of our capacity for receiving the most genuinely human messages. What he guessed about the press was that it was developing a new medium of publicity and advertising. True, technological development (e.g., "the speed of the printing press") might facilitate the spread of this medium of communication. Yet the real cause of its success, if it should succeed in becoming the most influential medium of the age, would be the willingness of people to hear the quality of message it gave. When people came to the stage of becoming bored with actuality and wishing to be entertained all the time with something more "interesting" than the truth, then this medium would become a drug to which, refusing all proper nourishment, they would become fatally addicted. The aesthetic mode would triumph and drive out both the ethical and the religious mode of understanding life.

It is indicative of the accuracy of Kierkegaard's statement that the leveling process is for us the equivalent of the classical concept of fate that we so readily acquiesce in the belief that technology creates new modes of apprehending the world by inventing new media of communication, rather than that human beings want to apprehend the world in a certain way and that they consequently develop new means of gratifying their wishes. There is a superstition abroad that humanity is carried along from one age to another and has only one duty: to be contemporary. This superstitious belief is the product of accepting, consciously or unconsciously, a theory of the evolution of consciousness that deifies the time stream. Kierkegaard's insight into what was happening in the nineteenth century gives an alternative and much more credible explanation, and one which puts human intentionality in the driver's seat instead of fate. We get what we want, because what we really want we work for, or persuade others to produce on our behalf. Kierkegaard did not think that publicity and advertising were absolutely new, in the sense that the human mind had never received the kind of messages they gave before. The newness was that never before had a whole society wished to guide itself by that kind of message. The contemporary proliferation of an advertising industry using every conceivable technological device seems to support his argument.

When Kierkegaard said that the press was an abstraction catering to the abstraction of the public he did not mean that men did not write advertising and publicity messages and that other men did not read what they wrote. He meant that neither writers nor readers were involved as individuals, but that the whole activity was carried out by people remaining in "the third person." Personal responsibility, the ethical mode of existence was avoided by a proclaiming a new "duty," namely "informing the public." But what was the quality of this information, and who exactly were to be informed? With an exaggeration needed to make a valid point, Kierkegaard answered that the "information" given was gossip, and "the public" was simply anyone and everyone who would buy newsprint in order to obtain gossip. The result was that the aesthetic category triumphed over existence, with tragic results when people made actual decisions on the basis of gossip, while the Press applauded and said that the public had shown what it really wanted. "Life's existential tasks," said Kierkegaard, "have lost the interest of reality" (P.A., 78).

We have only to consider the importance today placed on the "image" of a public figure to understand that Kierkegaard was scarcely setting up a straw man in order to knock it down. Not what is, but what publicity can make to seem plausible, may decide a nation's policy. The propaganda of a totalitarian state shows the lengths to which the manipulation of truth in the interests of an ideology may go and the devastating effect upon those who, believing lies, are then themselves ripe for manipulation. But the "rape of the masses" is a universal phenomenon and is not imposed only from above, as Kierkegaard understood when he said that the crowd is untruth.

Kierkegaard wrote, "The present age with its sudden enthusiasms followed by apathy and indolence is very near the comic" (P.A., 39). When President Kennedy was assassinated, millions saw the actual event on the T.V. screens of their living rooms, and presumably were "involved in depth." Yet, in spite of the immediate outcry for legislation to register firearms, nothing was done until the repetition of *actual events* of the same kind persuaded the conscience of the nation that action was acutely necessary. Being there "in the third person" produced only the reaction which Kierkegaard described—sudden enthusiasm followed by apathy.

Marshall McLuhan remarks that perhaps the editor's chair was the symbol of the nineteenth century, the psychiatrist's couch being the symbol of the twentieth. The chair, keeping the occupant in tension, encourages a "hot" response, while the relaxing freedom of the couch produces a "cool" atmosphere. McLuhan may be right, though one hopes not. "Hot" and "cool" have some relation to Kierkegaard's concepts of "passion" and "reflection in the hands of an abstract power." The editors of the press whom he castigated so mercilessly were not wholly given over to purveying gossip. They still respected existence enough to give their personal views and expected their readers to argue the issues "hotly." But those who lie on the psychologist's couch are those who cannot cope with existence, and argue only with themselves about the issues arising within their own reflective life. Folk wisdom has christened psychiatrists "headshrinkers." If the couch in their offices is indeed the symbol of the present age, then the reduction of life to the aesthetic mode which Kierkegaard talked about has really taken place. Our heads are not big enough to contain passion any longer. Inwardness has been replaced by the need to relay our private gossip to someone who, for a fee, will lend a sympathetic ear and tell us how, if we cannot find joy in living, we can at least escape falling into insanity and thus continue to preserve the semblance of an existing individual.

V

The Evaporation
of Existence

AFTER HEGEL THE SYSTEM that was to exhibit the Truth of the Whole came under attack for concentrating too much on the Whole to the neglect of the parts, particularly of the parts that interested us most nearly, namely, this earth and the people on it. So it happened that Kierkegaard's concern with existence was taken up in a way—though not in his way.

Marx brought the System down to earth with a bump, through the simple expedient of turning it upside down (the *right* way up, of course, from his standpoint). The Hegelian dialectic of Absolute Spirit became dialectical materialism. World history was no longer to be read as the story of self-estrangement being overcome through the perfection of self-consciousness, but was man's victory over the forces alienating him from his fellows and the good earth; while the culmination of the historical process was the unified perfection of a classless society instead of the unified perfection of Absolute Knowledge. System as such, nevertheless, remained enthroned. Like Hegel's System, you had to take it or leave it; it was the whole truth about the Truth of the Whole, or nothing.

Another attack upon the omnipotence of System as forceful as Kierkegaard's, though quite independent of his (no one imagined any good thinker could come out of Copenhagen!), was soon forthcoming. Schopenhauer had earned Kierkegaard's approval for his stress upon the will, and, while his thought remained systematic in intention, it gave the impression that, ultimate reality being irrational, man must stand by the actuality of his will to live. With Nietzsche the concept of System was utterly rejected as he moved beyond Schopenhauer to posit the finality of the individual's will to power. There was no evolutionary process spiritual or material (Darwin was beside the point) to be caught in the net of reason. The creativity of man was the sole justification for the belief that there can be meaning for the world, and that creativity must be built on the conviction that meaning cannot be found anywhere outside himself. Nor was man a given entity; he must make himself. For this reason Nietzsche looked for the coming of the Superman, the Higher Man who would show—*if* he came—what human existence could achieve.

When the philosophy of existentialism began to be talked about in connection with the names Heidegger, Jaspers, and Sartre, then Kierkegaard and Nietzsche appeared as major influences. It seemed then reasonable to conclude, as many did, that there was a philosophical position called existentialism which came, rather oddly, in two distinct types: the Christian and the atheistic. And so it might have been, had the philosophers in question aligned themselves behind one or the other of the two nineteenth-century thinkers. But this they did not do. Instead, they declared themselves indebted to both about equally. Yet Jaspers confessed himself a Christian, Sartre loudly proclaimed himself a militant atheist, and Heidegger (Sartre's inspiration and teacher) was assumed to be an atheist too, until he said that this had been a too hasty deduction from his writings by those who did not understand them.

Moreover, none of them accepted Kierkegaard's belief that affirming individual, concrete existence as the arena of human concern rules out the possibility of including existence in a speculative system. It is true that they all shunned the word "system," but each of them produced a philosophy which attempted to give a *unitary* explanation of what we need to know about reality. And that was precisely what Kierkegaard protested against in Hegel's System. None of them went Kierkegaard's way of saying that the existing individual accepts a truth that defies the reason to comprehend it, and, precisely because it cannot be comprehended, is existentially received as the truth.

When Kierkegaard put forward his two theses about a speculative system being possible and an existential system being impossible, he might as easily have said (had there been at the time a need for putting it in just that way) that an existential philosophy, unless it is a speculative system, is impossible. What he did say quite clearly is that existence is not put into a speculative system by adding a paragraph within the system that mentions the concept of existence. He could hardly have foreseen the time when nearly every paragraph of a system would discuss this concept (though he was certain that he would fall victim to "the professors" sooner or later). But had he done so, he would not have needed to alter his statement. Its point would still hold just as firmly.

Let me repeat Kierkegaard's point more directly. The existential is that which cannot be thought, only lived concretely by an individual. We can, of course, reflect upon this-which-cannot-be-thought, just as we can imagine a chocolate layer cake when we are hungry. But, once we claim that this reflection is what constitutes the truth of the existential, we have introduced a principle of mediation by means of which, Hegelian-fashion, contradictories have been reconciled. And to speak of existentialism is to make this very claim. We may think about the existential (as every existing individual does from time to time). That is a world away from thinking in terms of a philosophy called existentialism. If what is concrete is made into an abstract noun, then someone has been trying to get "beyond" the existential in order to carry that concrete thing into the speculative realm. And that is comic. Only the speculative thinker believes you demonstrate your recognition of the fact that the human body needs nourishment by saying that, whenever you imagine a cake, you imagine *a very solid one* having a double layer of chocolate frosting.

Since this is a study in Kierkegaard, and not in twentieth-century existentialism, it is obviously impossible to describe the various existentialist systems in turn in order to point out how the principle of mediation is introduced in each. A few pointers to the three well-known existentialists already referred to will have to suffice.

To begin with, the existentialism of "the present age" did not spring directly from Kierkegaard and Nietzsche. It came out of ground prepared by a succession of different attempts to prove, against an empiricism assuming that knowledge of reality can and must be gained by exploring the observed object and excluding the observing subject, that the subject may be all-important in coming to know reality. In the second half of the nineteenth century thinkers such as Windelband and Dilthey had contrasted the knowledge proper to the natural sciences and the knowledge sought by the human sciences, particularly by history. Then, in the phenomenology of Husserl, Heidegger's teacher, came an attempt to show how, by describing what we perceive immediately and without trying to interpret it ("a phenomenon") we can reach *pure consciousness in its own absolute Being.* Jaspers, Heidegger, and Sartre all employed from the first the phenomenological method. Although they have not supported Husserl's openly idealistic conclusions, the goal they have been intent to reach is indicated by their endorsement of the method.

An existentialism using the phenomenological method believes in the sole cogency of what Kierkegaard called a direct relation to the truth. This appears most clearly in Heidegger, who, because he emphasizes that his concern as a philosopher is with Being, has denied being an existentialist of any kind. His big book *Being and Time* was not called *Existence and Time,* he once observed. Yet, equally, Sartre's big book is called *Being and Nothingness: An Essay on Phenomenological Ontology* —although *he* insists that he is an existentialist. In Jasper's opinion, philosophy's function is to lead men to an awareness of Being and to their place in it. He used to speak of his philosophy as a philosophy of existence, but gave up doing so in 1950; after that he liked to speak of the philosophy of reason.

A review of Sartre's *Being and Nothingness,* written a few years ago by the astute philosopher and novelist Iris Murdoch, was given the title of "Hegel in Modern Dress." If we think in terms of Kierkegaard's "how" giving the essence of the "what," that motto might stand over the systems generally grouped together and labeled "existentialism." The difference in the "what," considered in detail, is substantial, while the difference in the "how" is all but negligible. The change brought about by putting Hegel in modern dress is rather like the change from the crinoline to the miniskirt: there is a lot less material and a different shape, but the principle of the thing remains the same.

Whereas Hegel believed that the Real lies open to Reason so that the two can be immediately seen to be one, twentieth-century existentialism thinks that alone in man's consciousness of the situation obtaining in his own selfhood is there direct access to reality. This strikes the eye at once in Sartre, whose theory of Being (ontology) rests on the sharp distinction between the being of things, the *en-soi* (the in-itself), and the being of man, the *pour-soi* (the for-itself). Yet this distinction goes back to Heidegger's setting apart of the human mode of being, *Dasein* (being-there, being-in-the-world) from the alternative mode of simply being *a* being. And both thinkers find the essential characteristic of human existence to reside in the capacity of man to relate himself to himself.

It takes no very great penetration to see that Kierkegaard's objection to the speculative thinker—namely, that he wishes to keep complete continuity in his thought at the expense of actual existence—has not been answered by this retreat from the comprehensiveness of Hegel's System. For what has been pushed to one side is the empirical world, and what has been placed in the center is the self-relatedness of human consciousness. Now Kierkegaard never denied the "objectivity" of the world—which was in fact the God-given locus of existence—but only the idolatrous preoccupation with the temporal that ignored (or thought it could ignore) the eternal. In relation to knowing the external world, he denied strenuously the attempt to produce an "objective" knowledge that was more than a probable hypothesis (he called this type of knowing "an approximation-process"). But he directed the main weight of his polemic not there, but against the speculative attempt to know objectively that which could only be known subjectively, i.e., existential truths concerning man's own inward realms of reason, freedom and faith. He characterized this type of thinking as trying to stand at one and the same time on both sides equally, saying that *this* type of thinking produced "the happy delusion of an imaginary I-am-I" of idealism. Yet it is precisely such a "happy delusion" that is evident in the modern existentialists' description of man's consciousness as the ability to relate himself to himself.

Jaspers illustrates admirably the "standing on both sides equally" syndrome. No one quotes Kierkegaard more often or with more fervor. Yet his philosophy of *Existenz* sets out to show that the thinker must press on to transcend the split between Subject and Object, which, Kierkegaard said, was the very embodiment of the fantastic and the comic in speculative thought. Jaspers proposes to achieve this supreme work of mediation by "elucidating the Comprehensive." "The Comprehensive" is a technical term meaning, as Jaspers tells us: on one hand, the being-in-itself surrounding us, and on the other, the being which we are. Jaspers does not believe that the Comprehensive can be presented conceptually, but must be explored through its various "modes" through which, if we persevere, we catch glimpses of the Transcendent, Being-itself, *God.*

It is important to note that Jaspers has his dialectic, one which, as has often been pointed out, seems to be the opposite of Hegel's. (The opposite, *I* would point out, does not mean the contradictory.) The reconciliation of what seems to be irreconcilable comes about for Jaspers chiefly when the contradictoriness of things tears us apart. So, for example, out of the experience of Nothingness we come to realize the presence of Being-itself. This happens when we are driven to extremes—to "boundary situations." It is only when the foundations we stand on are shattered, he finds, that we can see things as they really are, and find the strength to stand firm. As a result of his dialectic, Jaspers commends to his readers not a philosophy quite as objectively the Truth of the Whole as Hegel's, but one proposed for acceptance as a "philosophic faith."

Jaspers' dialectic has common tones with that of Heidegger and Sartre, who both link the mode of being of man with Nothingness. Since man is faced with the certainty of death all through his life he experiences *Angst* (dread), no ordinary anxiety but an indefinable one, said Heidegger. His earlier writings elaborated the theme with varying emphases, coming to the conclusion that Nothingness is not simply negation but actually a part of Being, so that when man faces his existence "authentically" he discovers Being. Sartre takes the same understanding of man's mode of being, being *pour-soi,* as Nothingness. But, going further, he identifies Nothingness with the Absolute. Man, making himself, chooses his own existence in utter freedom; yet it makes no difference what he chooses. The purposeless exercise of freedom is its own reward. "Man is the useless passion."

The idea of the choice of authentic existence leading to the discovery that Nothing becomes the place where Being is encountered (or, with Sartre, the place where man wills to stand in order to transcend the meaningless world and make his own meaning) seems to have close connections with the teaching found in *Either/Or* about winning through to existence by choosing oneself. Without any question, Kierkegaard's thought has been drawn upon—"pillaged," some commentators suggest, is the word. The existentialists have borrowed the stage Kierkegaard designed, together with its sets and actors. They have reconstructed the scene in which man walks alone, constantly shadowed by the threatening power of Dread, a monster that never shows its face. But they have changed the play. It is no use expecting to find the dialectic of either/or developed here, since Kierkegaard's bete noire, the dialectic of both-and, carries everything before it.

Looking back, then, over the development of philosophical existentialism in the first half of the twentieth century, we find that, for Jaspers and Heidegger, contradictories turned out to be agreeable bedfellows. In *Being and Time* Heidegger found in his *Dasein* the means of endorsing Hegel's doctrine of the identity of Pure Nothingness and Pure Being. He therefore left exploring man's being-in-the-world for the quest for metaphysics, just as Jaspers started from *Existenz* and arrived at a philosophy of reason. Sartre, from all appearances, remained faithful to the existential theme. Rejecting the synthetic path, he was content to let Nothingness stand alone. But appearances are hardly to be trusted. For Nothingness was not grounded in existence in Sartre's existentialism. The subjectivity of the existing individual did not decide anything, since everything had been decided beforehand by "objective" thinking. A Hegel-type speculative theory, relating Being and Nothingness, dictated the mode of man's being-in-the-world. What Kierkegaard said about the speculative thinker's comic stance, therefore, could be applied to Sartre's view that it is the "uprising of the *pour-soi* that brings it about that there is a world." In order to posit the "objective" world that has existence only in the Idea, the existing philosopher "absent-mindedly" cancels himself out, leaving his speculative construction floating between heaven and earth like Mohammed's coffin.

If the history of twentieth-century existentialism were ever to be made into a film, the title should surely be, "Whatever Has Happened to the Existing Individual?" In ontologies purporting to describe, with the help of Kierkegaard, the true mode of man's being, the existentialists gave us man-as-such, man viewed *sub specie aeterni.* Individual existence simply evaporated; and Kierkegaardian subjectivity, along with it, boiled away in the systematic pot on the speculative stove.

Existentialism is no longer the newest intellectual fashion around. It has been declared dead, buried, and forgotten by a number of pundits who are now advertising other lines of thought as better suited to contemporary tastes. Had Kierkegaard's thought really been taken up into the existentialism of the first half of the twentieth century, then we might be prepared to say that he does not promise us anything for the future. But, if the existentialism which is now beginning to look passé were actually a revival of the ideas against which he fought a century ago, then we ought to pay careful attention, at this stage of the game, to what he was saying then. It is just possible that postexistentialist thinking may preserve exactly those features of the Hegelian tradition that he exposed as highly questionable. As I have tried to show throughout the present study, changes in terminology do not necessarily mean a change in outlook. So a glance at the reasons why existentialism, regarded from a Kierkegaardian point of view, went astray should help us to see how Kierkegaard can guide our estimate of current trends in the world of ideas.

The speculative approach to life, in Kierkegaard's eyes, was unrealistic and misleading because it never looked beyond the aesthetic mode of existence. The wholly aesthetic orientation of existentialism has been brilliantly analyzed by the Danish Lutheran theologian Regin Prenter, in an article entitled "Sartre's Concept of Freedom Considered in the Light of Kierkegaard's Thought."[1]

While Dr. Prenter examines Sartre only, and then at one point of his thinking—his concept of freedom—his conclusions have a much wider application. He points out that Sartre's notion of man choosing to exist by continually negating what he is, in order to become what he is not as yet, has no connection with Kierkegaard's notion of the self that chooses its own eternal validity. Yet it resembles exactly the Kierkegaardian description of the way the aesthete chooses (or rather fails to choose) in a desperate effort to revolt against the conditions of existence. The Dread which Sartre believes to be the constant companion of the free man, revealing the Nothingness of his mode of being and the futility of all his choices, is described by Kierkegaard as the slavery of the person who, since he never rises above the aesthetic, on that account becomes the victim of chance, change, and despair, "the sickness unto death." Such slavery may be regarded by the despairer as proof that "he wills himself." It is proof only that he has spurned the goodness of existence (S.U.D., 207).

Interestingly, the same description of the despairer is applied to Heidegger by F. H. Heinemann in his book *Existentialism and the Modern Predicament.*[2] Dr. Heinemann is looking at the later stage in Heidegger's thinking when, wishing to get "beyond" metaphysics (a good Hegelian ambition in itself, surely), he goes in Dr. Heinemann's judgment "through defiance into absurdity," and thus qualifies for the title of Kierkegaard's despairer, the man driven on toward the final despair of defiance.

The rejection of existentialism came to a great extent from the feeling that the existentialist attitude—especially the posture of defiance in the face of a "meaningless" universe—led to absurdity and nowhere else. It has often been pointed out that existentialism was nourished by the European experience of catastrophe in two World Wars and of terror under totalitarian regimes. North America was never exposed in the same way to life in these "boundary situations," and consequently never responded wholeheartedly to the concepts of Dread and the Absurd. The American Way of Life, i.e., the goals of middle-class American society, seemed thoroughly defensible until the late fifties.

The sixties brought a striking change in mood, leading to a wide rejection of these goals. On the one hand, the protest took the form of "dropping out," and on the other of "engagement." Diverse as these ways seem, I think they show, once again, how opposites are not contradictories. The traditional American ideal of freedom to seek self-fulfilment survives. Only now there are fresh routes being proposed to realize the ideal. The movement that began with the beatniks and gave birth to the hippies assumes that the external freedom of the old-style rugged individualism of the frontier can be achieved in the sterile megalopolitan environment only internally. The city is a new wilderness to be subdued by a new-style ragged individualism. Here officialdom is the Indian raiding party to be held at bay, and suburbia takes the place of the Eastern seaboard of an effete culture to be escaped at all costs. In the psychedelic outposts Mark Twain's words live again: "Soap and [career] education are not so sudden as a massacre, but they are more deadly in the long run." Over against the escapees from the Great Society stand those who remain within it to demand, through group action, a society that will be actually organized for government of the people, for the people, and by the people. They find the present state of America very like that of Colonial days, with the Establishment a King George III, an alien oppressor.

The dropouts represent pure aestheticism. (The revival of *art nouveau,* the product of late-nineteenth-century art-for-art's-sake theory, is significant.) Drugs, of course, are subjective freeways for bypassing existence. Even the more socially acceptable phenomenon of the discothèque, with its "total environment" of sound and color and movement, dissolves the individual into Kierkegaard's "animal hysteria." (The demoniacal, he observed, is essentially musical—Dru, 165). No doubt hippiedom will fade away, although some solemn social observers—the heirs of Kierkegaard's "professors"—have proclaimed it the preview of the culture of the future. The social protesters are more likely to be laying the foundations of a new pattern of community living.

But is existence being fostered better by those who contract *in* than by those who contract *out?* Kierkegaard believed the strong-minded self intent on action to have some consciousness, though an abstract one, of its spiritual self (S.U.D., 201-02). Yet, through lack of ultimate seriousness, this self will founder through not accepting its own limits. Certainly, history shows example after example of the idealistic revolution-

[92]

ary becoming the cynical politician, the conscienceless power worshiper. For Kierkegaard the crucial question is always whether we rise above the aesthetic, where we wish to make the internal or the external world conform to our whims, to the ethical-religious, where we place our individual existences behind our dreams and our actions. The alternative is either nihilistic destructiveness or else "sudden enthusiasms followed by apathy and indolence."

Today we are always being urged to be "contemporary," to get "with it." Yet the "it" is an abstraction, and the "contemporary" does not exist. "Contemporary man" is a speculative construction—"the public" reified. We are told likewise that we must adapt to a world where there will be more changes in the next twenty years than in the past two thousand. Yet the biggest change of all is perennial: the concrete moment when the living individual changes into a corpse. If our lives are to be more than a succession of disjointed "contemporary experiences" without content, we must face the concrete moment ethically. That is Kierkegaard's reminder to us, individually. Only thus, he tells us, can we gain continuity. We must come out of the crowd and reveal ourselves. This is existence. This is *gaining a history* (C.U.P., 227). Speculating about world history, the progress of mankind, our duty to the future, and so forth, is—twaddle. Argument about what man is going to be, and how best to get ready for the future, avoids ethical decision now.

There can be no existence, says Kierkegaard, without ethics. The last sentence of *Either/Or* ends with the words "only the truth which edifies is truth for you" (E/O, II, 294). Much is said just now about concern for "persons" and about the need for building a "responsible community." At the same time, the vital link between person and community—the institution of marriage—is widely regarded not to be an ethical responsibility essentially, but rather to be a matter of personal happiness. So compatibility becomes the prime requisite in choosing a partner, and "mental cruelty" grounds for seeking divorce. Choice is oriented, therefore, to common tastes; and taste is the Kierkegaardian aesthetic norm. No ethical choice can be predicated upon taste.

Kierkegaard began his work of witnessing to the reality of existence by pointing out in *Either/Or* that the first step away from the aesthetic to the ethical is the transcending of the erotic in an individual's commitment to the married state. For this is where we pass from the "possibles" that will never be realized in existence (as our divorce statistics today confirm) to actuality. We find freedom only through a realistic acceptance of limits. Only the aesthete wants to abolish limits, because, having no determinate self, he dreams of unlimited possibilities. The existing self finds its infinite freedom in existential choice, i.e., ethically. The limit is our charter of liberty to be ourselves. Thus our ethical responsibility to humanity, the generation of the children of men, does not begin with feelings of universal benevolence.[3] It begins with one specific choice made with earnestness and pathos. Marriage, with its commitment of the individual for his entire existence, is such an existential choice; and parents who have never found what it means to live "in the strength of the ethical" cannot pass on to their children the knowledge of what it means to be a self. Life is not a game where we make up the rules as we go along, it is being "educated by reality"—turning to, and not away from, existence.[4]

VI
The Direct Speech of Christianity

"THE ETHICAL REALITY of the individual is the only reality," says Kierkegaard (C.U.P., 291). For here is the breach with immediacy, with the aesthetic. Here, when an existing individual discovers inwardness and subjectivity, the self is posited as spirit. But this means that, experiencing the passion for the infinite, he is faced with the religious. The individual knows that existential choice is always made *before God*. "His self is, as it were outside of him, . . . because he chooses it absolutely out of the hand of the eternal God" (E/O, II, 182).

Man, a synthesis of the temporal and the eternal, is never without spirit. Until the breach with the immediate occurs, however, spirit is not posited. In *The Concept of Dread* this thesis is applied to paganism and Judaism. Paganism "upon the whole is sensuousness," while Judaism rises to consciousness of guilt (C.O.D., 86, 92). Only Christian faith holds the answer to the question of sin and guilt, in Kierkegaard's view, and it is an answer involving suffering. So *The Concept of Dread* ends with the statement that the concept must be handed over to Christian dogmatics (C.O.D., 145); and the content of Christian revelation, as it relates to salvation from sin and guilt, is expounded in *Philosophical Fragments*.

Kierkegaard believes that, since Christianity came, it is no longer possible to reinstate the aesthetic "sensuousness" of paganism in its innocence of the consciousness of guilt, although this is continually being attempted, because men want to avoid the "severity" of Christianity.

Kierkegaard's argument has been brought to life in our own day in the person of Albert Camus. Camus, though he stood very close to Sartre and other French existentialists through his involvement in the Resistance Movement of World War II, did not become an existentialist. He felt himself drawn to the Greek view of life (referring with feeling to "the sunny Mediterranean heritage"). Like the Greeks, though, he could never put out of his mind the cold cemeteries that lie behind the beaches where bathers bask in the warmth of the sun. Enraged by the contradictions of life, he compared man's state to that of Sisyphus in the Greek myth. (For offending the gods, Sisyphus was condemned eternally to push a heavy rock uphill, only to see it roll back again). Yet, in spite of himself, he wished to bring the Christian ethic of responsibility and compassion into the Absurd. He argued with Christian belief, accusing it of preferring dogma to concern for human misery; yet, behind his accusations there was sympathy and even admiration. In his last book, *The Fall,* his debate with Christianity was brought to a more intense pitch, though not resolved. *The Fall,* as its title indicates, was entirely preoccupied with the themes of guilt, remorse, and the possibility of atonement.

Compared with Camus, Sartre's attitude to Christianity is dogmatically polemic. He insists that this existentialism is, first and last, an atheism intent on proving the God-is-dead proposition. This he understands in terms of Nietzsche's belief that man must "kill" God in order to make himself man. Killing God is man's first duty to himself.

This God-killing motif in Sartre's and Nietzsche's thinking is one clearly directed to denying the reality of the Christian God (and not just any God), because the Christian God demands obedience as well as belief, repentance as well as faith. Christianity preaches an ethical center lying outside man. The will of the Creator has decreed what *existence shall be,* and so what *man must do.* Thus killing God means wiping the memory of a religion positing sin from the modern consciousness. Now, Kierkegaard did not live to read Nietzsche, but he knew the kill-the-Creator motif from the literature of romanticism in the early nineteenth century. With romanticism, new life was given to the Greek myth of Prometheus, the defier of Zeus the Father God; and, with it, to the medieval story of Faust, who sold his soul to the devil in order to gain power on earth. (Faust, Don Juan, and the Wandering Jew—all rebel figures—fascinated Kierkegaard in his university days when romanticism was at its height). Nietzsche and Sartre continued this Romantic tradition.

Romanticism is usually understood as the protest of feeling against reason, of vital energy against restricting formalism, and of the inner truth of the imagination against the rules of logic and the mechanistic "laws" of science. Kierkegaard was influenced by romanticism. (It is often credited with inspiring him to champion "passion" and "subjectivity"—and possibly also to rebel against the Father-Rule of the National Church). Yet he saw that romanticism was the aesthetic attitude made into a religion. It was the attempt to have the "poetic" engulf existence. He attacked it in *Either/Or*.

Poetry, for Kierkegaard, is the realm of the possible, its sphere being not existence but words. It gives to airy nothing a local habitation and a name. The poet's words are true in that they represent true possibilities he has known subjectively. Subjectivity is truth. Only through our consciousness can we know *anything*. But objectivity also is to be sought, for it is the source of truth—truth beyond our imaginings, truth that is given us to know through our encountering it. This the romantic overlooks. Living on the poetry that is in him, he fails so to develop his subjectivity that it shall become objective. Only a poet who has a tenacious regard for actuality (e.g., Shakespeare) is able to "let the objective prevail" in his poetry. The romantic is the man who has never sufficiently trusted his own subjectivity to discover that man does not live by words alone.

Kierkegaard's understanding of the romantic fallacy has wide application to the field of religion and religious substitutes. It applies to the willing-the-death-of-God program of

Nietzsche and Sartre and their successors. It is easy for us to kill a God who threatens our imagined possibilities. He can be killed instantaneously—in words. But it is equally easy to bring into being—in words—a God who flatters our poetic omnipotence and never breathes a word about sin and guilt. We have only to extend imagined possibilities to discover the Absolute, the end of every possibility. This Absolute is readily given a habitation within us. Man can imagine himself God, since imagined possibilities laugh at logical or existential contradictions. The aesthetic thinker freely unites the Infinite with the Finite (Hegel), Being with Nothingness (Heidegger), Freedom with Necessity (Marx), and Heaven with Hell (William Blake in *The Marriage of Heaven and Hell*). In the aesthetic realm the speculative thinker is a poet, too, though not nearly so clever at handling words. In his study of Blake, *The New Apocalypse*,[1] Thomas Altizer finds that Blake's thought and Hegel's are much alike—a fact that would not have surprised Kierkegaard. That speculative thinkers are not too dexterous, though, in poetic expression is indicated by the record of Hegel's and Heidegger's complaints that no one ever really understood them!

Both the romantic and the speculative thinker, in Kierkegaard's view, want to be pagans. Paganism fits the world of abstract possibilities. But Christianity is not poetry; it is anchored in history. Moreover, it denies the immediacy that the pagan consciousness assumes to qualify the relation between the divine and the human. It says that man cannot know the truth about himself and his situation in existence unless God reveals this to him (the argument of *Philosophical Fragments*). It says that its message is an Absolute Paradox to be grasped subjectively in faith, not a speculative truth to be grasped "objectively" or immediately (the argument of the *Postscript*). Finally, it says that its message will be rejected both by the aesthete and pagan or postpagan romantic, and by the leveled-down public in Christendom, living on a diet of indifferentism and trust in technical progress to solve all human problems. Neither is willing to face existence long enough to allow individual recognition of sin and guilt. Neither knows the passion of inwardness that imitates the suffering existence of Christ (the argument of *Training in Christianity* and of the writings constituting the *Attack upon Christendom*).

It would seem that Kierkegaard's teaching had made hardly a greater impression upon the theological world than it has upon the philosophical one, in spite of the enthusiasm aroused by the "discovery" of his authorship. Well, he himself expected no better of our age than sudden enthusiasms . . . .apathy and indolence. At least, he would not claim he has never been understood. He said he was a poet speaking about religion. The public took the poetry gladly enough, but did not want the religion. Will was lacking, not understanding. To speak about Christianity, its severity and its gentleness, was his work. If he said what he had to say plainly, that was all he could do—as a poet. His existence was between him and God.

It is tempting to think of making a Kierkegaardian critique of several of the "schools" of contemporary Christian thought, especially of those that have "pillaged" Kierkegaard's expressions (mostly via Heidegger). But, in order to limit the field, I shall simply try to bring Kierkegaard's views on Christianity into relation with one very influential figure on the modern scene: Dietrich Bonhoeffer.

Bonhoeffer is best known for the stimulus he has given to thinking about the place of Christianity in today's world through his theme of "religionless Christianity." On the face of it, there seems a complete contradiction between Bonhoeffer's wish to make Christianity religionless and Kierkegaard's wish to introduce people to the religious category so that they might be able to know what Christianity was. Nevertheless, I believe their total intention to have been either identical or complementary. If Bonhoeffer's thinking opens a new era in Christian theology, as many are convinced it will, then Kierkegaard's influence on us may be just beginning.

There are a few parallels between the careers of the two

[99]

thinkers. Both were Lutherans, both loved literature and philosophy, yet were, first and last, Christian thinkers; both made a name for themselves early, both died early, and both were most influential some time after their deaths. In temperament and life story they were, however, entirely different: the one so narrowly confined, the other so far-ranging and engaged in world affairs. These differences tend to flatten out, maybe, when we think how each followed to the end a path he believed to be not of his own choosing. Each loved company, and was forced to know solitude. Each had hoped for a normal family life, and had to leave it for another calling. Each spoke of "the cost of discipleship" in the same terms: Commitment, Suffering, and Joy. In the "how" of their living their lives the same "what" was given.

It is paradoxical that Bonhoeffer struggled to find "a secular interpretation of biblical concepts," yet never succeeded in doing so. Kierkegaard came to his solution of the same problem early, when he took over Hegel's language and adapted its terminology to convey the message of the New Testament. Today we fail to recognize this obvious fact, since Hegelian terminology no longer dominates our intellectual world. For his day, Kierkegaard was "radically contemporary." In this direction, he wished as much to be "worldly" as Bonhoeffer ever did.

Also, in his understanding of Christianity, Bonhoeffer's antispeculative polemic was all Kierkegaard could have desired it to be, though his language, suiting altered times, was very different. But, chiefly, Bonhoeffer's stress upon the "how" of Christianity related him to Kierkegaard.

What Bonhoeffer means by "religion" is precisely what Kierkegaard took to be the misunderstanding of Christianity current in Christendom. In the *Letters and Papers from Prison*,[2] Bonhoeffer asks what it means to "interpret in a religious sense," and answers his own question thus: "I think it means to speak on the one hand metaphysically, and on the other hand individualistically" (156). Kierkegaard could have endorsed that statement entirely, since the first point is his objection against speculation, "objective" thinking, and the second has nothing to do with *being* an individual but with what Kierkegaard named the twaddle bandied about in Christendom about Christianity being "consolation, happiness, etc." and calling forth "Sunday tears." Kierkegaard's view of what it means to be an individual finding truth in subjectivity is precisely described in Bonhoeffer's "Outline for a Book" in the *Letters:*

> What do we really believe? I mean believe in such a way that we stake our lives on it? The problem of the Apostles' Creed 'What *must* I believe?' is the wrong question (210).

Succinctly stated, this is Kierkegaard's theme of the "what" being given only in the "how."

Even Bonhoeffer's concern for not wanting to persuade a world "come of age" to return to religion would have had Kierkegaard's approval. One of the latter's constant desires was to have Christianity preached *against;* since, otherwise, no one could distinguish the genuine article from the spurious. Bonhoeffer believed that the passing of a universal but theoretical belief in *a* God might mean "opening up a way of seeing the God of the Bible," the only way to faith being "through repentance, to *ultimate* honesty" (196-7; Bonhoeffer's italics). Kierkegaard wrote that he would support a man's right to rebel against Christianity, if only the rebel knew how he stood in relation to faith, for: "Honesty is what I want, and wherever there is honesty I can take part" (A.U.C., 39). Over the passing of Christendom as Bonhoeffer saw it, the waning of the "religious premiss," Kierkegaard would have shed no tears.

The root of the matter, though, is in the common agreement of both thinkers about the essential nature of Christian faith as a "given," not to be evaporated by equivocation with words. Christianity for the two of them was the God-Man, Jesus Christ, the Absolute Paradox, demanding our faith.

This "given" is a constant theme throughout Bonhoeffer's writings. In the *Letters* it appears most clearly in his rejection of Bultmann's "typical liberal process of reduction" in stripping off the "mythological" elements of Christianity to reduce it to its "essence." Wrote Bonhoeffer:

My view is that the full content, including the 'mythological' concepts, must be kept—the New Testament is not a mythological clothing of a universal truth; this mythology (resurrection etc.) is the thing itself—but the concepts must be interpreted in such a way as not to make religion a precondition of faith (181-82).

Nothing could be more in line with Kierkegaard's fundamental thinking. For Bonhoeffer's "liberal process of reduction" read Kierkegaard's "logical transcription of Christianity, transferring it into the sphere of the intellectual," and for "not to make religion a precondition of faith" read "not a doctrine but an existential communication," and then the statement is Kierkegaard's own. Bonhoeffer's belief that "this mythology (resurrection etc.) is the thing itself" is Kierkegaard's fighting challenge: "The object of faith is hence the reality of the God-man in the sense of his existence" (C.U.P., 290).

A detailed comparison between Bonhoeffer and Kierkegaard all along the line would be interesting. Bonhoeffer appreciated Kierkegaard, particularly in his understanding of how in Lutheranism the acceptance of justification by faith as doctrine had resulted in the illusion of "cheap grace." (Kierkegaard said the doctrine was used as a fig leaf behind which people skulked in a most unchristian way!) Because of his positive attitude to the Old Testament, Bonhoeffer had a higher estimate of the worth of "natural" life than had Kierkegaard; though even here his concept of living "completely in this world," namely, throwing ourselves utterly in the arms of God and watching with Christ in Gethsemane (*Letters*, 201-02), sounds very Kierkegaardian. But, since Bonhoeffer's wish for a nonreligious interpretation of Biblical terminology has been widely assumed to mean that the Gospel must be *irrelevant* unless it is recast into terms *meaningful to contemporary man,* I shall end my investigation by

[102]

considering why it is that Bonhoeffer and Kierkegaard alike insist upon a "given" in Christianity that no interpretation can alter without losing "the thing itself."

Kierkegaard's authorship was undertaken in the first place in order to convince people that Christianity was not irrelevant. The concept of irrelevance, we should note, is either subject to formal definition (e.g., the irrelevant in a law court is what does not comply with the rules of legal evidence); or else it is a personal judgment at work, and one usually geared to the aesthetic norm of *taste*. "Irrelevance!" is the aesthete's magic word to make the ethical disappear. That their "solution to the Jewish problem" was an inhuman enormity was irrelevant to the Nazis. That he is already married is irrelevant to the man who has convinced himself that his new love is a beautiful experience. Kierkegaard knew how hard it is to touch people drugged with an aesthetic vision they believe to be objective truth. Somehow they must be persuaded to submit to education by reality. Otherwise they will never discover the subjective route to the objective. Instead, they will demand that reality fit into their ready-made aesthetic categories and theoretical systems. Anything resisting this treatment is dismissed as irrelevant.

Kierkegaard's "speculative thinkers" and Bonhoeffer's "liberals" are such categorizers and system makers. In his *Letters* Bonhoeffer accused these thinkers of using God to solve their problems, or of wanting to clear a space for religion in the world. Their method was to say that it was not *real* religion that was irrelevant, but only an outmoded type, one meaningless to modern man because it contradicted his understanding of the universe. Bonhoeffer insisted that this contradiction cannot be removed from Christianity, because you cannot "separate God and miracle" (156). Here he took up Kierkegaard's theme that Christianity is what speculative reason will never understand, since speculative reason remains in the immanent. Clearing a space for religion in the world means emasculating Christianity. For Christianity lies in the "beyond" that is more than metaphysical transcendence, the infinite in our mind.

Being content with a Christianity we can understand is paganism, according to Kierkegaard. The existentialist-ontologists cling tenaciously to the idea of a direct relation of the divine to human consciousness. Transcendence reveals itself in boundary situations as the Encompassing (Jaspers); or man exists in the neighborhood of Being, where the gods reveal themselves (Heidegger). The principle of mediation, so fundamental to speculative thinking, thus annuls the "beyond" and brings it into a space in the world.

Because of Kierkegaard's polemic against objective thinking, the term "experienced non-objective reality" has been coined—plainly another name for the same thing, and a perfect example of Kierkegaard's thesis that speculation delights in uniting contradictories. In 1839 Mynster combated the proposition that rationalism, naturalism, and supernaturalism were outdated concepts and now must be reconciled in a wider synthesis. Mynster said—and Kierkegaard warmly approved—that contradictories could not be mediated. Yet recently we find Bultmann writing in an essay on "The Idea of God and Modern Man": "The contrast between here and beyond, and thus the contrast between naturalism and supernaturalism, must be overcome. God must be recognized as the Unconditional in the conditional."[3] Progress! Heidegger, at least, sees that his viewpoint calls for a return of "the gods" he finds invoked by the Greeks and by the romantic poets. He does not identify the Being of which man is (as he likes to say) "the shepherd" with the God of the Bible who is man's Shepherd. Yet Heidegger's thought, both early and late, is widely proposed as the basis for a valid contemporary Christianity.

If Christianity was not to be paganism warmed over, Kierkegaard insisted that it must be accepted by the individual in subjectivity, i.e., in faith. There was no direct route from our consciousness to the New Testament Gospel, because the Gospel posits a relationship that is existential, not speculative. (Today we would have to add: not existentialist-ontological, either.) The aesthetic consciousness reads the Unconditional in the conditional out of the resources of its own self-understanding. The New Testament tells us of God's relating himself to us in the existence of the God-Man. This is an Absolute Paradox to the understanding, but for the existing individual it is objective truth received subjectively. It is, in New Testament terminology, foolishness to the Greeks but God's wisdom to those who are called to know Christ (1 Cor. 1:23-24).

In receiving Christianity, we received objective truth on its own authority, Kierkegaard believed, in place of so-called objective thinking. In 1837 he wrote in his *Journals:*

> All other religions are oblique. The founder stands aside and introduces another speaker, they themselves therefore come under religion—Christianity alone is direct speech (I am the truth) (Dru, 166).

The direct speech of Christianity will not commend itself to the speculative understanding, which will try to turn it into general truths. It will call this speech "mythology" (Bultmann), or "religious symbol" (Tillich), or "ciphers of transcendence" (Jaspers), or "being encountered by the word event which becomes the source of the understanding of word events" (Gerhard Ebeling). Then speculation will proceed to make the New Testament yield "meaningful" propositions about human consciousness. (The "I am the truth" of John 14:6 will become a summons to us to understand our existence authentically, or to recognize essential God-Manhood, or to experience Transcendence through one of the modes of the Encompassing, or to find *through* language that we share the nearness of Jesus to God.) Never once will it suggest that Christian faith should accept New Testament language as a statement about the God-Man himself.

Already in his Christology lectures of 1933[4] Bonhoeffer had argued that "liberal" theology understood Jesus solely as the support for, or embodiment of, certain ideas, values, or theories; but that the "incomprehensibility" of the person of Jesus Christ could not be changed into something comprehensible. In the *Letters* he wrote (213):

> The key to everything is the 'in him.' All that we may rightly expect from God, and ask for, is to be found in Jesus Christ. The God of Jesus Christ has nothing to do with what God, as we imagine him, could do and ought to do. If we are to learn what God promises, and what he fulfils, we must persevere in quiet meditation on the life, sayings, deeds, sufferings, and death of Jesus.

We have here the justification for, and indeed the statement of, Kierkegaard's concept of the Leap.

The existentialists who have "pillaged" Kierkegaard have always been drawn up short here. Kierkegaard, they say, was escaping from reality, causing reason to abdicate, retreating into the incredibility of the supernatural, and in general behaving shockingly. But for Kierkegaard the Leap (he took the word from Lessing) is the very heart of the existential way, because it is the evident characteristic of existence to be discontinuous.

Of course, accepting Christian faith looks, from the angle of speculative thinking, like a sellout. It is just that. It leaves behind the fantastic stance of the abstract thinker. It *laughs* at his vain attempt to draw the universe out of his head, and set it dancing to the tune of his paltry pipe. (Humor, in fact, is our preparation for the rigors of the religious sphere.) The individual, leaping from the comprehensible to faith, takes the subjective way to find the objective, and declares that he accepts the direct speech of the New Testament as reality. He may be wrong. But, if he is, it will not be because speculation has proved him wrong. It will be because Christianity is not, in reality, the truth. He may be right—if Christianity proves to be the truth it has always claimed to be. At least, he will not have mistaken Christian truth for what it is not and never was. He will not have sold his Christian birthright for a mess of nonexistent pottage.

Epilogue:
The Promise of Kierkegaard

KIERKEGAARD'S OWN HOPE was that his reflections upon Christianity would make obvious to the least reflecting mortal that faith was "not a class for numskulls in the sphere of the intellectual, or an asylum for the feeble minded" (C.U.P., 291). He hoped, incidentally, to arouse people to the misuse of words that was poisoning thought.

The promise of Kierkegaard for our day lies in the fact that these are just the two lessons we need most to learn now. Theology in Christendom was never more abstract, jargon-laden, and split into groups (none of which seems able to communicate with the rest) that rise and disappear like moving shadows. Meanwhile, there is so little conviction of faith being a challenge to the intellect that the cry goes up on all sides, prophesying that Christianity must die unless it can learn to conform to the prevailing thought patterns.

Kierkegaard is one who shows us that the idols of the present age, Contemporaneity, Change, and Relevance, are "by nature no gods," as Paul once told the Galatians concerning the then current deities. We worship abstractions, ignoring existence; until, like old Firs in *The Cherry Orchard,* we find life has slipped by and we have never lived.

Only a very few, said Kierkegaard, are capable of receiving an impression of reality. We might try, though, to be of that company.

Notes

Chapter I. The Crucible of the Authorship

1. London: Harvill, 1948.
2. Cf., for example, Walter Lowrie, *A Short Life of Kierkegaard* (Princeton, N.J.: Princeton University Press, 1942), pp. 27ff.
3. Cf. Louis Dupré, *Kierkegaard as Theologian* (New York: Sheed & Ward, 1963), pp. 25ff.: also John Updike, "The Fork," a review of Kierkegaard's *The Last Years, Journals, 1853-1855,* edited and translated by Ronald Gregor Smith (New York: Harper & Row, 1965) in *The New Yorker,* February 26, 1966, pp. 115-36.

Chapter II. The Strategy of the Dialectic

1. The title was a typically cryptic reference to the author's belief that he would die at thirty-four.
2. In his *Lectures on the Philosophy of Religion* Hegel said of the promise made to Eve by the serpent that Adam and she would be like God, knowing good and evil:. . . "the serpent does not lie. God Himself confirms its words."

Chapter III. Reflection on Existence

1. See the Select Book List. Especially useful is *Kierkegaard's Authorship: A Guide to the Writings of Kierkegaard* by George E. Arbaugh and George B. Arbaugh (Rock Island, Ill.: Augustana College Library, 1967). This is a painstaking commentary following the works chronologically. Of first-rate importance, because of the new material it makes available in English, is the collection of Kierkegaard's incidental writings now being translated and edited by Howard V. Hong and Edna H. Hong, assisted by George Malantschuk. In this multivolume work the entries are arranged

alphabetically under subject headings instead of by date. The first volume of the Hongs' work has been published: *Søren Kierkegaard's Journals and Papers*, Volume 1, A-E (Bloomington, Ind.: Indiana University Press, 1967).

2. Princeton, N.J.: Princeton University Press, 1968.
3. Herbert M. Garelick's *The Anti-Christianity of Kierkegaard: a Study of* "Concluding Unscientific Postscript" (The Hague: Martinus Nijhoff, 1965) argues that the *Postscript* tries to be too rational about the irrationality of faith. Garelick concludes (p. 71): "Climacus' movement, however, is imperfect. Making Christianity a means, not an end, he violates the absoluteness of religion. In attempting to show the Paradox as the absurd and the irrational, he succeeds only in making Christianity a good gamble. The Postscript is a stage to be overcome in the movement to Christianity." The fallacy of this argument consists in trying to assimilate the stance of Climacus to that of Lessing, or (to say the same thing differently) to wish to be objective about the subjective—to try to view the subjective *sub specie aeterni*. The category of "a good gamble" is a speculative one completely excluded when subjectivity is taken seriously; and any recommendation of Christianity on such *quantitative* terms must be one made "without earnestness."

Interlude: Pause for Looking Around

1. *Sub specie aeternitatis,* "under the aspect of eternity," is the usual form of this Latin phrase, which has become known through Spinoza's use of it as a prominent concept in his philosophy. Kierkegaard regularly used this other form, which gives the meaning "under the aspect of the Eternal," i.e., *as God sees.* He deliberately introduced the personal reference.

Chapter IV. The Age of the Crowd

1. To "get 'beyond' " is a Hegelian term, which is why Kierkegaard used it here.
2. Recorded in the *Journals* is an intriguing story of how Kierkegaard had decided to scrap the Preface, but retained it at the request of the compositor; causing Kierkegaard to think that perhaps he had found "that individual" in a man one would normally have imagined to be bored by just another manuscript (Dru, 430).

3. Quoted by Howard A. Johnson in "Kierkegaard and Politics" (*A Kierkegaard Critique,* edited by Howard A. Johnson and Niels Thulstrup. New York: Harper & Brothers, 1962), p. 79. The article is of great interest and one of the best introductions to its subject.

Chapter V. The Evaporation of Existence

1. Translated by Margaret Grieve and H. R. Harcourt in *A Kierkegaard Critique,* pp. 130-40. Another translation by Harris Kaasa, "The Concept of Freedom in Sartre Against a Kierkegaardian Background," has appeared in *Dialog,* Vol. 7, Spring 1968, pp. 132-37.
2. New York: Harper & Row (Harper Torchbooks), 1958, p. 108.
3. Bernard Shaw's epigram "Do not do unto others as you would that they should do unto you. Their tastes may not be the same" shows the comic result of reducing the ethical to aesthetic terms.
4. John Updike's novel *Couples* (New York: Alfred A. Knopf, 1968) is to some extent an up-to-date *Either/Or.* The couples spend their time playing games, and the losers are their children.

Chapter VI. The Direct Speech of Christianity

1. Subtitled *The Radical Christian Vision of William Blake,* East Lansing, Mich.: Michigan State University Press, 1957.
2. Third edition, revised and enlarged. London: S.C.M. Press, 1967, or New York: Macmillan.
3. Translated by Robert W. Funk in *Translating Theology into the Modern Age* (New York: Harper & Row, 1965), pp. 82-95. The passage quoted is on p. 91.
4. *Christ the Center,* New York: Harper & Row, 1966.

Key to Abbreviations

Books (numerals in text refer to page numbers)

A.U.C.:   *Attack upon Christendom, 1854-1855*
C.I.:   *The Concept of Irony*
C.O.D.:   *The Concept of Dread*
C.U.P.:   *Concluding Unscientific Postscript*
E.D.:   *Edifying Discourses*
E/O: *Either/Or; a Fragment of Life*
F.A.T.:   *Fear and Trembling*
O.A.R.:   *On Authority and Revelation; The Book on Adler*
P.A.:   *The Present Age*
P.F.:   *Philosophical Fragments*
P.O.V.:   *The Point of View, etc.*
S.U.D.:   *Sickness unto Death*
T.I.C.:   *Training in Christianity*

*Other
Writings*   (numerals in text refer to numbered entries)

Dru: *The Journals of Søren Kierkegaard*
Hong: *Søren Kierkegaard's Journals and Papers*

Bibliography

Kierkegaard's Works in English

Attack upon Christendom, 1854-1855. Tr. Walter Lowrie. Princeton, N.J.: Princeton University Press, 1944.

Christian Discourses. Tr. Walter Lowrie. London: Oxford University Press, 1940.

The Concept of Irony; with Constant Reference to Socrates. Tr. Lee M. Capel. New York: Harper & Row, 1965.

The Concept of Dread. Tr. Walter Lowrie. Princeton, N.J.: Princeton University Press, 1944. (2nd ed. entitled *The Concept of Anxiety.*)

Concluding Unscientific Postscript. Tr. David F. Swenson and Walter Lowrie. Princeton, N.J.: Princeton University Press, 1941.

The Crisis in the Life of an Actress. Tr. Stephen Crites. New York: Harper & Row, 1966.

Edifying Discourses, I-IV. Tr. David F. Swenson and Lillian Marvin Swenson. Minneapolis: Augsburg Publishing House, 1943-1946.

Either/Or: a Fragment of Life. I-II. Tr. David F. Swenson, Lillian Marvin Swenson and Walter Lowrie. Princeton, N.J.: Princeton University Press, 1946.

Fear and Trembling. Tr. Walter Lowrie. Garden City, N.Y.: Doubleday & Company, 1954. (This edition, a Doubleday Anchor Book, also contains *The Sickness unto Death.*)

For Self-Examination. Tr. Edna and Howard Hong. Minneapolis: Augsburg Publishing House, 1940.

The Gospel of Our Sufferings. Tr. A. S. Aldworth and W. S. Ferrie. Grand Rapids: Wm. B. Eerdmans Publishing Company, 1964.

The Gospel of Suffering and *The Lilies of the Field.* Tr. David F. Swenson and Lillian Marvin Swenson. Minneapolis: Augsburg Publishing House, 1948.

Johannes Climacus, or De Omnibus Dubitandum Est. Tr. T. H. Croxall. London: Adam and Charles Black, 1958.

Judge for Yourselves. Tr. Walter Lowrie. Princeton, N.J.: Princeton University Press, 1944.

On Authority and Revelation: the Book on Adler, or a Cycle of Ethico-Religious Essays. Tr. Walter Lowrie. Princeton, N.J.: Princeton University Press, 1955.

Philosophical Fragments: or A Fragment of Philosophy. Tr. David F. Swenson; 2nd ed. rev. Howard Hong. Princeton, N.J.: Princeton University Press, 1962.

The Point of View, etc. Tr. Walter Lowrie. London: Oxford University Press, 1939.

The Present Age and *Of the Difference Between a Genius and an Apostle.* Tr. Alexander Dru. New York: Harper & Row, 1962.

Purity of Heart Is to Will One Thing. Tr. Douglas V. Steere. New York: Harper & Brothers, 1956.

Repetition. Tr. Walter Lowrie. Princeton, N.J.: Princeton University Press, 1941.

The Sickness unto Death. (See *Fear and Trembling.*)

Stages on Life's Way. Tr. Walter Lowrie. Princeton, N.J.: Princeton University Press, 1940.

Thoughts on Crucial Situations in Human Life. Tr. David F. Swenson and Lillian Marvin Swenson. Minneapolis: Augsburg Publishing House, 1941.

Training in Christianity. Tr. Walter Lowrie. Princeton, N.J.: Princeton University Press, 1944.

Works of Love. Tr. Howard V. Hong and Edna H. Hong. New York: Harper & Row, 1962.

The Journals of Søren Kierkegaard; A Selection. Tr. Alexander Dru. London: Oxford University Press, 1938.

The Last Years: Journals 1853-1855. Tr. Ronald Gregor Smith. New York: Harper & Row, 1965.

Søren Kierkegaard's Journals and Papers, I, A-E. Tr. Howard V. Hong and Edna H. Hong, assisted by Gregor Malantschuk. Bloomington, Ind.: Indiana University Press, 1967.

Select List of Books about Kierkegaard

Arbaugh, George E., and George B. Arbaugh. *Kierkegaard's Authorship: A Guide to the Writings of Kierkegaard.* Rock Island, Ill.: Augustana College Library, 1967.

Collins, James. *The Mind of Kierkegaard.* Chicago: Henry Regnery Co., 1953.

Croxall, T. H. *Kierkegaard Commentary.* New York: Harper & Brothers, 1956.

Dupré, Louis. *Kierkegaard as Theologian; The Dialectic of Christian Existence.* New York: Sheed & Ward, 1963.

Johnson, Howard A. and Niels Thustrup, editors. *A Kierkegaard Critique: An Inter-National Selection of Essays Interpreting Kierkegaard.* New York: Harper & Brothers, 1962.

Lowrie, Walter. *Kierkegaard.* Two volumes. New York: Harper & Brothers (Harper Torchbooks), 1962.

———. *A Short Life of Kierkegaard.* Princeton, N.J.: Princeton University Press, 1942.

Malantschuk, Gregor. *Kierkegaard's Way to the Truth: An Introduction to the Authorship of Søren Kierkegaard.* Tr. Mary Michelsen. Minneapolis: Augsburg Publishing House, 1963.

Rohde, Peter P. *Søren Kierkegaard: An Introduction to his Life and Philosophy.* Tr. Alan Moray Williams. New York: Humanities Press, 1963.

Additional List of Books about Kierkegaard

Blackham, H. J. *Søren Kierkegaard (1813-1855).* London: Routledge and Kegan Paul, 1952.

Bonifazi, Conrad. *Christendom Attacked: A Comparison of Kierkegaard and Nietzsche.* London: Rockliff Pub. Corp., 1953.

Brandt, Frithiof. *Søren Kierkegaard, 1813-1855.* Tr. Ann R. Born. Copenhagen: Danish Information Office, 1963.

Carnell, Edward J. *The Burden of Søren Kierkegaard.* Grand Rapids: Wm. B. Eerdmans Publishing Company, 1965.

Chaning-Pearce, M. *The Terrible Crystal.* London: Routledge and Kegan Paul, 1940.

———. *Søren Kierkegaard.* London: James Clarke & Co., Ltd., 1948.

Cochrane, Arthur C. *The Existentialists and God.* Philadelphia: Westminster Press, 1956.

Collins, James. *The Existentialists.* Chicago: Henry Regnery Co., 1952.

Croxall, T. H. *Kierkegaard Studies.* New York: Roy Pubs., 1956.

Diem, Hermann. *Kierkegaard: An Introduction.* Richmond: John Knox Press, 1966.

Eller, Vernard. *Kierkegaard and Radical Discipleship.* Princeton, N.J.: Princeton University Press, 1968.

Friedman, Maurice. *The Worlds of Existentialism.* New York: Random House, 1964.

Friedmann, Rudolph, *Kierkegaard.* London: Peter Nevill, Ltd., 1949.

Garelick, Herbert M. *The Anti-Christianity of Kierkegaard: A Study of* "Concluding Unscientific Postscript." The Hague: M. Nijhoff, 1965.

Gates, John Alexander. *The Life and Thought of Kierkegaard for Everyman.* Philadelphia: Westminster Press, 1960.

Grene, Marjorie. *Introduction to Existentialism.* Chicago: University of Chicago Press, 1959.

Griffith, Gwilym. *Kierkegaard.* London: Lutterworth Press, 1943.

Haecker, Theodor. *Kierkegaard, the Cripple.* London: The Harvill Press, Ltd., 1948.

———. *Søren Kierkegaard.* London: Oxford University Press, 1937.

Harper, Ralph. *The Seventh Solitude: Man's Isolation in Kierkegaard, Dostoevsky, and Nietzsche.* Baltimore: Johns Hopkins Press, 1965.

Heinecken, Martin. *The Moment Before God.* Philadelphia: Muhlenberg Press, 1956.

Heinemann, F. H. *Existentialism and the Modern Predicament.* New York: Harper & Brothers, 1958.

Hubben, William. *Four Prophets of Our Destiny.* New York: The Macmillan Company, 1952.

Jolivet, Régis. *Introduction to Kierkegaard.* London: Frederick Muller, Ltd., 1950.

Martin, Harold Victor. *Kierkegaard, the Melancholy Dane.* New York: Philosophical Library, 1950.

———. *The Wings of Faith.* New York: Philosophical Library, 1951.

Michalson, Carl, editor. *The Witness of Kierkegaard.* New York: Association Press, 1960.

Pelikan, Jaroslav. *From Luther to Kierkegaard.* St. Louis: Concordia Publishing House, 1950.

Price, George. *The Narrow Pass; A Study of Kierkegaard's Concept of Man.* New York: McGraw-Hill Book Co., Inc., 1963.

Roberts, David. *Existentialism and Religious Belief.* New York: Oxford University Press, 1957.

Ruggiero, Guido de. *Existentialism.* New York: Social Sciences Publishers, 1948.

Sponheim, Paul. *Kierkegaard on Christ and Christian Coherence.* New York: Harper & Row, 1968.

Swenson, David F. *Something about Kierkegaard.* Minneapolis: Augsburg Publishing House, 1949.

Thomas, J. Heywood. *Subjectivity and Paradox.* New York: The Macmillan Company, 1957.

Thomte, R. *Kierkegaard's Philosophy of Religion*. Princeton, N.J.: Princeton University Press, 1948.
Untermeyer, Louis. *Makers of the Modern World*. New York: Simon & Schuster, 1955.
Wild, John. *The Challenge of Existentialism*. Bloomington, Ind.: University of Indiana Press, 1948.
Wolf, Herbert C. *Kierkegaard and Bultmann: the Quest of the Historical Jesus*. Minneapolis: Augsburg Publishing House, 1965.
Wyschogrod, Michael. *Kierkegaard and Heidegger*. New York: Humanities Press, 1954.
Zuidema, S. U. *Kierkegaard*. Nutley, N.J.: Presbyterian & Reformed Pub. Co., 1960.